MEDITATION FOR MODERN MADNESS

Meditation for Modern Madness

HIS EMINENCE THE SEVENTH
DZOGCHEN RINPOCHE,
Jigme Losel Wangpo

FOREWORDS BY

Dodrupchen Rinpoche and Alak Zenkar Rinpoche

Wisdom

Wisdom Publications
132 Perry Street
New York, NY 10014 USA
wisdomexperience.org

Library of Congress Cataloging-in-Publication Data
Names: Jigme Losel Wangpo, Dzogchen Rinpoche VII, 1964– author.
Title: Meditation for modern madness /
    His Eminence the Seventh Dzogchen Rinpoche, Jigme Losel Wangpo.
Description: First edition. | New York: Wisdom Publications, 2024. |
    Includes index.
Identifiers: LCCN 2023055155 (print) | LCCN 2023055156 (ebook) |
    ISBN 9781614299486 (paperback) | ISBN 9781614299721 (ebook)
Subjects: LCSH: Rdzogs-chen. | Meditation—Rdzogs-chen. |
    Spiritual life—Buddhism.
Classification: LCC BQ7662.4 .J524 2024 (print) | LCC BQ7662.4 (ebook) |
    DDC 294.3/444—dc23/eng/20240220
LC record available at https://lccn.loc.gov/2023055155
LC ebook record available at https://lccn.loc.gov/2023055156

ISBN 978-1-61429-948-6   ebook ISBN 978-1-61429-972-1

28 27 26 25 24
5 4 3 2 1

Cover design by Marc Whitaker/MTWdesign. Interior design by Gopa & Ted 2, Inc.

Printed on acid-free paper that meets the guidelines for permanence
and durability of the Production Guidelines for Book Longevity
of the Council on Library Resources.

Printed in Canada.

Contents

Foreword

BY H. H. DODRUPCHEN RINPOCHE

FOLLOWING the heartfelt requests from the students of His Eminence the Seventh Dzogchen Rinpoche, Jigme Losel Wangpo, I, the Fourth Dodrupchen Rinpoche, Thupten Trinley Palzang, offer these humble prayers for *Meditation for Modern Madness*.

May this book help spread the profound teachings of the Great Perfection in the ten directions, and may the indestructible qualities of Dzogpachenpo flourish and overcome all adversity.

I beseech all who practice Dzogchen to follow the advice of the authentic lineage holder, Dzogchen Rinpoche, and hold his pith instructions within your hearts. Practically applying the wisdom of Dzogchen and prioritizing the spiritual in everything you do is the greatest offering, benefitting all.

It is my sincere wish that *Meditation for Modern Madness* brings spontaneous great peace to all sentient beings. May they be liberated from the suffering of mind for this and all future lifetimes.

May these words bring the blessing of Padmasambhava and all the lineage masters to all who read them.

His Holiness the Fourth Dodrupchen Rinpoche,
Thupten Trinley Palzang
Sikkim, 2021

Foreword

BY H. E. ALAK ZENKAR RINPOCHE

THIS BOOK by His Eminence Dzogchen Rinpoche is offered in the manner of a gift for the entire Dzogchen lineage and is a must-read for Buddhists in general and for Buddhist scholars whose motivation, minds, and goals are vast. The purpose of this introduction is to draw attention to the tremendous blessings and great strength of the magnificent practitioners of Dzogchen of the past, such as the master Patrul Rinpoche and others, and especially to the deep, profound, and extraordinary Dzogchen *Khandro Nyingthig* and the like. Above all, it is to establish the preeminent place of the great Dzogchen Rinpoches who have appeared throughout the history of the Dzogchen lineage. In their golden age, it was not necessary to guide or give instructions in Dharma and meditation to Dzogchen practitioners.

Now, this precious primordial awareness and discriminating intelligence of the Dzogchen lineage, which is supreme from the beginning, is being disseminated here for students in the contemporary world in clear language that can be felt, understood, and easily applied.

The author of this book, the lord protector, the most excellent His Eminence the Seventh Dzogchen Rinpoche, is the reincarnation of His Eminence the Sixth Dzogchen Rinpoche, Jigdrel Jangchub Dorje, who appeared in the fortunate age of attainment. He imparted Dharma and bestowed the empowerments, transmissions, and so forth of the Nyingma tradition from within the prestigious Dzogchen Monastery in Kham, eastern Tibet, and its surrounding areas.

A spiritual master and scholar such as the present Dzogchen Rinpoche, who has experience in meditation and practice and is free from clinging and attachment to the eight worldly concerns, is extremely rare in these times.

That kind of pure, untainted conduct is so joyful and uplifting to me; it is worthy of respect and veneration. It is my intense wish that the extensive activities of the present Dzogchen Rinpoche will be beneficial for the joys and sorrows of the entire spectrum of sentient beings, and that the conduct of the past and present Dzogchen Rinpoches, which is free from clinging and attachment, will continue to flourish and spread for years to come. So be it.

His Eminence the Second Alak Zenkar Rinpoche,
Thubten Nyima
Chengdu, Sichuan, Peoples Republic of China, 2022

Editors' Preface

THESE TEACHINGS of His Eminence the Seventh Dzogchen Rinpoche, Jigme Losel Wangpo, address the reader in a very personal, practical, and direct way. His explanations and advice come directly from the experience and realization of Dzogchen, the Great Perfection, which has been passed down directly from master to disciple since the time of the Buddha. This direct transmission is the definition of a living spiritual lineage. Dzogchen Rinpoche was recognized as the incarnation of the Sixth Dzogchen Rinpoche at a young age by His Holiness Dodrupchen Rinpoche and is the holder of this lineage.

Dzogchen Rinpoche demonstrates his great skill by sharing these ancient teachings as practical methods that are directly applicable and supportive of our modern lives. As Westerners, we often regard spiritual practice and meditation as out of touch with the world, something that doesn't really fit into our lives and can only be practiced with an abundance of time and effort. We also believe that their goal lies somewhere in the distant future. Rinpoche shows us how our everyday lives can be turned into spiritual practice, not only easing our stress but also allowing the true nature of our minds to reveal itself, right now, on the spot.

Dzogchen Rinpoche is the holder of the *Khandro Nyingthig* lineage, the "Heart Essence of the Dakinis," which Guru Rinpoche received from Shri Singha and then entrusted to Princess Pema Sal before concealing it as a terma. The *Khandro Nyingthig* terma was discovered many years later by the princess's rebirth, the terton Pema Ledrel Tsal, at Daklha Tramo Drak rock. Her next rebirth was the omniscient Longchenpa, who ensured the authentic lineage was kept alive. Dzogchen Rinpoche is the living embodiment of the *Khandro Nyingthig*, and his teachings remain as pure and unaffected by external influences as they were during Guru Rinpoche's time.

As students of Dzogchen Rinpoche, having experienced the tremendous benefit and blessings of the Dzogchen teachings in our own lives, we have long awaited the opportunity to share them with a larger audience, but it is only recently that Rinpoche has given his permission to do so. We are honored and delighted to be able to publish this book. May you enjoy your reading.

Editorial Team

Preface

THE ANCIENT wisdom of Dzogchen has been kept isolated for many years in the Himalayas, without being connected to the lay community. That has been a little bit frustrating for me. I remember saying twenty years ago, "We have to break this habit and connect it to the people who really need these teachings." Western students have very busy and stressful lives, with family obligations, jobs, kids, and mental and physical stress of all kinds. Dzogchen is the excellent teaching for this sort of time and for this sort of people, rather than the monks in the monasteries, who have a very easy life already. They have received an overload of teachings, while the lay community hasn't had access to the teachings at all for a long time. I was told, "Oh, they don't need that, they won't understand it." I thought this was a little bit odd, which is why I decided, around fourteen years ago, to change that. I said, "I'm going to teach Western people to understand this, it's very important for them. They should have access to philosophy, meditation, and rituals. They should all have access."

It's a great opportunity that laypeople, particularly in Western societies, have access to the Buddhist teachings, particularly to Dzogchen. Dzogchen is very simple compared to other teachings. You don't need to spend thirty years in a monastery to learn it. I don't think you have that time. You may have time to go into retreat for five days a year, or for two weeks a year, or something like that, but you have your jobs and family commitments for the rest of the time. How will you find lasting happiness and enlightenment in that short period of time?

This can only be attained through Dzogchen, nothing else. I am introducing this simple and quick method because it is very, very practical and everyone can practice it. You simply need to recognize the great potential that is naturally born within everyone. You are already enlightened. You don't need to get enlightened again or to make your enlightenment better. It's not something you have to create or believe in. You just need to recognize who you already are. It's quite simple.

His Eminence the Seventh Dzogchen Rinpoche,
Jigme Losel Wangpo

Acknowledgments

I dedicate this book to my family: to my wife, Vicky; my three sons, Tsewang Rinzin, Orgyen Rigzin, and Jamyang; and my two daughters, Tara and Saraswati. I would like to thank them for their constant support and encouragement, which has been a continuous source of inspiration for me. I would also like to thank my editorial team, Gemma, Dorothee, Dee, Mark, Angelika, and Agnes. It has always been my wish to publish a book about the ancient wisdom teachings of Dzogchen to make them accessible to a more general readership. I also wrote it to remind myself of the precious Dharma so that it continues to be of benefit to me. The Dzogchen teachings encompass all the Buddhist vehicles and nothing that's been said here is meant to criticize any other tradition.

Introduction

The Dzogchen lineage is the lineage of Guru
Padmasambhava, who was also from India. This is also
the root lineage of the Nyingma, the original translation
school that came from India to Tibet.

AN ANCIENT LINEAGE

I WANT TO introduce the subject of meditation not just from my own crazy mind but from the ancient lineage of Dzogchen. In the Tibetan language, *dzog* means perfection and *chen* means great, so *Dzogchen* means Great Perfection. It is an ancient form of common sense. India gave rise to the most excellent spiritual wisdom over 2,500 years ago and the Dzogchen lineage is part of that wisdom. It came from India, was brought to Tibet, and continues to this day. This lineage originated with Gautama Buddha and was extremely successful at meditation, philosophy, and ritual.

People came from all over the world to study the Buddha's teachings at Nalanda University in northern India from the fourth to the twelfth centuries. It was a very important center of learning, the biggest university of its day. Nalanda didn't just teach philosophy; it taught medicine, science, astrology, geomancy, and martial arts at many different levels. Buddhism spread to many parts of Asia from Nalanda University. While most countries kept only parts or pieces of the Buddhist canon of teachings, Tibet retained everything completely. Buddhism has this long history and we are following this great lineage from India.

The Dzogchen lineage is the lineage of Guru Padmasambhava, who was also from India. This is also the root lineage of the Nyingma school, the original translation school that came from India to Tibet. *Nyingma* means old, not old in the sense of being rotten but in the sense of being an ancient lineage. Sometimes old can be good; old is not necessarily bad. In this sense, it is the oldest translation of the Buddhist teachings to come from India to Tibet. Therefore, we call it the Nyingma, the old or oldest lineage.

The Nyingma school has six monastic seats in Tibet: at Katok, Dorje Drak, Palyul, Mindrolling, Dzogchen, and Shechen monasteries. Dzogchen is the highest view in this school. It's the most precise and the most powerful lineage of teachings, while at the same time the most simple as possible. Dzogchen does not say you are going to get spiritual realization sometime in the future—you can experience it on the spot, you can get the taste of it now rather than three hundred or three million years later, in a distant lifetime. It is quite simple and straightforward.

The Incarnation Line of the Dzogchen Rinpoches

The Dzogchen Rinpoche incarnation line goes back almost four hundred years to Pema Rigdzin, who in 1685 founded Dzogchen Monastery in Kham, the easternmost province of Tibet. Pema Rigdzin became known as the Dzogchen Rinpoche, the personification of the Great Perfection teachings, because of his extraordinary realization and spiritual wisdom. One of his teachers said, "I have known Dzogchen as a teaching, but I had never seen Dzogchen as a person until I met you." Since that time, all the incarnations of Pema Rigdzin have been known as the Dzogchen Rinpoche.

The First Dzogchen Rinpoche, Pema Rigdzin, lived during the time of the Fifth Dalai Lama. They met in Lhasa, and the Dalai Lama requested he go to the eastern part of Tibet and build a monastery to establish the

Dzogchen lineage and the Dzogchen teachings there. This was a request from the Fifth Dalai Lama and, at the same time, a kind of prediction. That is what we call "a great sign." Pema Rigdzin and his three disciples, known as the sun, moon, and stars—Nyima Drakpa, Namkha Osel, and Rabjam Tenpai Gyaltsen—went on pilgrimage to Kham. The master and his three disciples traveled a bit like Aussie backpackers. Their backpacks were made of cane that were like two U shapes and they put their blankets and clothes in there. They eventually came to a valley in eastern Tibet. When they arrived where the monastery is now, in Rudam, they sat down to rest. They took their backpacks off and had a cup of tea. They usually traveled like pilgrims, that was their style.

They sat down there and performed a *serkyem* offering ritual. A serkyem is a silver bowl filled with fruits and biscuits, with a cup filled with what we call the "golden drink," which is offered to the local deities and protectors. After they had completed the protector's serkyem offering, a raven came down, picked up the serkyem in its beak, flew off, and dropped it. They decided to build the monastery on the very spot that the raven dropped the serkyem and asked the nomads to give them this land. Pema Rigdzin's backpack left an imprint in the rock where he put it to rest that can still be seen today. The First Dzogchen Rinpoche performed this miracle, leaving the imprint of his backpack.

The whole history of the Dzogchen lineage was built from that humble beginning. It's incredible. This lineage has produced so many branches and so many masters, it has spread in all directions. Dzogchen Monastery, with its 360 branches, became the biggest learning center; it was the second biggest Buddhist university in the entire world after Nalanda University, with around 980,000 monks. It developed all these great masters in the Nyingma, Kagyu, and Sakya traditions. It was very accomplished in ritual, meditation, and philosophy and produced a great many masters. Dzogchen Patrul Rinpoche, who wrote *The Words of My Perfect Teacher*, belonged to Dzogchen Monastery. His meditation cave is just behind the *shedra*, the school for monastics. Many other lineage masters came to learn from him, and his teachings created a branch lineage. The root lineage of Dzogchen Monastery is our lineage, the Dzogchen lineage. So many khenpos, so many great scholars and great masters were produced from Dzogchen Monastery shedra called Dzogchen Shri Singha Shedra. We also established many other shedras in the Kagyu and Sakya traditions. Many of the new young Nyingma khenpos in India are disciples of the Dzogchen lineage khenpos.

The Second Dzogchen Rinpoche, Gyurme Tegchog Tenzin, was born in Mongolia and was invited to come back to Dzogchen Monastery in Tibet. Thirty Mongolian families came to Dzogchen Valley with him. His Mongolian family was called Tsangpo Tsang. There have been generations of monks at Dzogchen Monastery that have descended from these Mongolian families, among them Venerable Genyen Rangjung, who would later serve the Fifth and Sixth Dzogchen Rinpoches.

The Third Dzogchen Rinpoche, Ngedon Tenzin Zangpo, wrote the commentary for Longchenpa's *Khandro Nyingthig*. This is comparable to Patrul Rinpoche's *Words of My Perfect Teacher*, which is a commentary on Jigme Lingpa's *Longchen Nyingthig*. Ngedon Tenzin Zangpo's commentary is a very direct introduction, a powerful fast track to understanding the view and practice of the *Khandro Nyingthig*. Thirty-seven of Ngedon Tenzin Zangpo's disciples attained rainbow body during their lifetime by following these teachings. This commentary was almost lost during the Communist invasion of Tibet, when all our Buddhist texts were burned. Only a single copy survived and found its way to Sikkim. We were able to reproduce the book in India from that copy.

The Fourth Dzogchen Rinpoche, Mingyur Namkhai Dorje, lived during the founding of Shri Singha Shedra at Dzogchen Monastery. The landscape of the shedra looked like the golden fish symbol, and when it was established, it is said Shri Singha flew from China to bless it. The first khenpo to graduate Shri Singha Shedra was Singtuk Pema Tashi, and the founder of the shedra was Gyalse Shenpen Taye, an emanation of Shantideva and a disciple of the Fourth Dzogchen Rinpoche. Shri Singha Shedra was blessed by Mipham Rinpoche and Patrul Rinpoche. Even Jigme Lingpa gave his blessings from afar, and when he did so, flowers rained down on it.

Then we experienced a few obstacles. The monastery was completely burned down in an accident. There was also an earthquake while the Fourth Dzogchen Rinpoche was visiting another monastery to bring back teachings and other transmissions. He put his robe over his head and said, "Oh, oh, oh, I have to protect, I have to protect, I have to protect." He moved his head and body, and the monastery stopped shaking. He could see what was happening from that distance. Everybody said it was kind of a shock to meet the Fourth Dzogchen Rinpoche because he was like a living buddha. Even the Dzogchen lineage masters would just go and touch his feet, he was such a powerful, incredible master.

The Fifth Dzogchen Rinpoche, Thupten Chokyi Dorje, rebuilt Dzogchen Monastery after the fires. When he started to rebuild the monastery, he asked all the forest deities and the local deities, "Please give us the logs and trees that we need to rebuild the monastery." The local deities offered the trees. He made this request because we cannot just cut down trees without their permission. Dzogchen Monastery really flourished during this period, and Shri Singha Shedra became very famous. The Fourth Dzogchen Rinpoche's realization had been very special, but he didn't create much structure at the monastery. It was left to the Fifth Dzogchen Rinpoche to bring everything at the shedra into good order.

Do Khyentse Yeshe Dorje and so many different masters visited at that time. Later, the retreat center at Dzogchen Monastery was also blessed by Jigme Lingpa. The whole place—the shedra and retreat center—were very blessed, but the retreat center was not as successful as Shri Singha. The location that had been chosen for the retreat center and blessed by the masters was changed due to monastery politics, and the result was not so auspicious. That's how it is sometimes. Though the blessing by Jigme Lingpa was still very powerful.

This Fifth Dzogchen Rinpoche is also famous for having recognized many of the great masters of the last century. His Holiness Dodrupchen Rinpoche, Penor Rinpoche, and even the Sixteenth Karmapa were recognized by him, which makes him the main authority for infallibly recognizing incarnations. Everyone who was recognized by him was an extraordinary master.

The Sixth Dzogchen Rinpoche, Jigdrel Jangchub Dorje, passed away at twenty-five years of age, during the turmoil of the Chinese invasion. He would have been the same age as the present Dalai Lama had he survived. This Dzogchen Rinpoche was very close to the Fourteenth Dalai Lama. The relationship between Dzogchen Monastery and the Tibetan government was very good. Dzogchen Rinpoche was invited to Lhasa by the Tibetan government and given the title of *hutuktu*, a rank of great spiritual significance that was second only to the king.

During the Chinese invasion of Tibet, Dzogchen Monastery was again burned down. Thousands of Chinese soldiers came, and thousands of monks and hundreds of tulkus and khenpos were locked together inside the monastery. Every time someone tried to get free, the army shot them. One of the top Chinese military officers was killed there and the army took his ashes back to China. The Chinese soldiers realized they were never going to defeat the Tibetans there, so they poured gasoline over the houses and the entire monastery and burned thousands of soldiers and thousands of monks to death. The monastery was completely razed to the ground. Some people tried to grab Dzogchen Rinpoche and other masters and help them escape. Dzogchen Rinpoche attempted to escape disguised as a Chinese soldier but was stabbed by one of his own monks who did not recognize him.

One old monk from Dzogchen Monastery managed to escape from Tibet to Sikkim. He told us all this history, otherwise we wouldn't know what had happened there. After the Chinese takeover, we were unable to receive any information for over twenty-five years—there was no crossing the border at all, so we had no idea what was going on. When the border reopened in 1983, the stories started being shared again. I received an invitation to return to Tibet in 1984 and made plans to visit my monastery and many of its branches. When I went to Tibet in 1985, the official story was that the military did not destroy my monastery, it had just burned down. But a lot of Chinese soldiers died there, too. Not to mention, the Sixth Dzogchen Rinpoche was stabbed to death and many people were shot as they resisted. I heard that everybody was riding around on horses doing phowa and dying on their horses. It was quite shocking to imagine how many people died near the monastery; thousands of soldiers and thousands of monks were killed. During my visit, I couldn't sleep. While I had thought the area would be full of spirits and ghosts, even though I couldn't sleep, it was very peaceful there because the land was so blessed.

THE SEVENTH DZOGCHEN RINPOCHE

The Seventh Dzogchen Rinpoche is me. I am called Jigme Losel Wangpo. I have two names: when I was nine, His Holiness Dodrupchen Rinpoche gave me the name of Jigme Losel Wangpo, and then after the age of twelve, I was invited to Dharamsala by His Holiness the Dalai Lama, who gave me the name of Tenzin Jigdral Lhunpo. When I was young, I had another name, but I can't remember what it was now.

It's important I share my own background and experience so that you know who I am and why I've written this book. I was born as the Dzogchen lineage holder, even though it wasn't something I chose for myself as a child. The lineage just put me in that position. I had to study with very serious masters and try to take responsibility for the lineage, in order to protect the authentic lineage and prevent it from being misused. It is my responsibility to maintain the lineage; that is my role. I try my best, but this is a very difficult task in the twenty-first century. It is a big challenge.

A lineage is something that is passed from master to disciple. Only when the disciple becomes accomplished can he or she pass the lineage on to someone else. We call this "transmission." At Nalanda University in ancient India, the transmissions were kept very confidential and protected. They would never be passed on to someone who did not have the view needed to understand them. That was the way to protect and maintain the lineage. We lost everything, but we did not lose the lineage. We lost the buildings, we lost the property, we lost the people, but the lineage is not lost, the transmissions are not lost, the culture is not lost.

I was recognized as the Seventh Dzogchen Rinpoche by His Holiness Dodrupchen Rinpoche in Sikkim. He is the incarnation of both Jigme Lingpa and Do Khyentse and is very important for the Nyingma lineage as the holder of the Longchen Nyingthig. The seventh Dodrupchen Rinpoche was regarded as the living Guru Rinpoche. His monastery is a branch of Dzogchen Monastery in Kham. Dzogchen Monastery is the mother monastery that maintained meditation, philosophy, and ritual in the Kham and Amdo regions of Tibet.

I was born in Sikkim, in northern India. When some of the older senior khenpos came to India we started a new Dzogchen Monastery, with a new history, in southern India. We were guided by His Holiness Dudjom Rinpoche, Dilgo Khyentse Rinpoche, and His Holiness the Dalai Lama. Everybody said, "Yes, you need to build this," and they gave us the direction needed to do so. We reestablished Dzogchen Monastery under my leadership with the help of my late father.

Dzogchen, known as *atiyoga* in Sanskrit, is the spiritual background of this book. The Nyingma tradition has nine different stages and atiyoga is the ultimate one. It is the highest wisdom of Tibetan Buddhism. Dzogchen has become a bit trapped by intellectual views in recent years, and it has been hard to maintain the lineage during the last few decades, but we have succeeded so far. There are a lot of things to do in Buddhism—endless philosophical texts to study and rituals to practice—and there is nothing wrong with that, but in Dzogchen, our practice is so simple, we almost do nothing.

While we need a way to maintain the lineage, Dzogchen has nothing to do with being part of a monastic tradition. It's just a very simple practice for everyone. It can be exercised and practiced in everyday life, such as on the levels of family, work, administration, and so on. It can help you improve your health, maintain your relationships, balance your emotions, and reduce your stress. In time, you will see the value of your life increase further and further; the purpose of your life will become clearer and everything will make more sense.

I had a great opportunity to study and practice Dzogchen, starting in my childhood. I was trained by this lineage to become a kind of model for the lineage, to guide and lead and protect the lineage. I had no choice—they put me in that position as a lineage holder, though since then I have never promoted myself as a great lama or master. When I was around seven or eight years old, I was taken from my family and formally recognized at the Seventh Dzogchen Rinpoche. The enthronement was held in the palace of the royal family of Sikkim. I had no idea what was happening; they sat me on a throne and put a huge traditional hat on my head. The hat was so big it almost covered my whole face. In the end, they had to make it smaller to fit my head. That hat was given to me by the head of the Nyingma school, His Holiness Dudjom Rinpoche. I still have it. It is okay now; it fits quite well.

PART 1

Why Meditate?

CHAPTER 1

Our Great Potential

*We all have buddha nature, the wisdom that is born with us,
has been with us all the time, and traveled with us from the
beginning—we just have never recognized it.*

LIFE'S BIG PROJECT

W E NEED to understand why each one of us was born. We didn't
just pop up somewhere for no reason; there is a significant purpose for us in having been born a human being. Interestingly, most of
the time we don't recognize this. We simply think, "Okay, I'm just here,
and that's it." But it's not like that, not at all. How can you make your
life more fun, more meaningful, and more purposeful? You need to recognize your great potential. We were not born as human beings just to
do something very basic and then spend our lives doing that until we are
close to death. That would be a great pity.

If you sit down and really look at yourself, you will see that each of
us has so much great potential, but we build limits around ourselves
and this great opportunity—this responsibility for, and possibility of—
achieving great things goes unrecognized. We have a big project, the biggest project of our lives: our enlightenment project. We need to make
a choice about the kind of life we want now and in the future. That life
doesn't depend on politics, fashion, or social media. It depends on you.
The choice is yours. Your freedom is yours; your future is yours.

Buddha Nature

It's important to understand that we are all equal because we all have a mind. We can have different types of minds—some are a little happy, some are a little grumpy, and some are kind of so-so. First, we need to recognize. What do we recognize? The great potential that is naturally born within everyone. We call this potential "buddha nature," but buddha nature has nothing to do with being a Buddhist. We assume that buddha belongs to Buddhism, but buddha is quite independent of the religious tradition of Buddhism. Similarly, Dzogchen has nothing to do with being religious. Religious views usually encourage us to think there is something wrong with us, that we need outside help to make ourselves better as people. Dzogchen tells us that all sentient beings have buddha nature—it doesn't matter how old or how young you are, what color, class, race, or gender you are; we are all equal because we all have this great potential, this incredible true nature. You have an incredibly precious and pure awareness within you. It's amazing, it's perfect. And it is there right now.

Some other Buddhist traditions might say that you're not good enough as you are, that you have to become something else—that you have to become a buddha. Dzogchen doesn't say you must become a buddha. You are *already* buddha. You are perfect from the beginning; you don't become perfect later, you don't change into someone better. In Tibetan, this is called Kuntuzangpo, the primordial buddha that is the personification of our own fundamental goodness. In Dzogchen, we never say that you are good on some days and not good on others. You are pure from the beginning, you just don't recognize it. If you can recognize who you are, that's it. How simple is that? The issue is that you are confused about your own nature; you find it difficult to accept because of the habit of mind that says, "No, I'm not good enough, I'm not a buddha; I'm a flawed human being." You always go back to this habitual mind. That's why you don't accept your buddha nature.

The way to recognize your buddha nature is through meditation. Wherever there is a mind, buddha nature is there. Whether you believe it or not, it is always there, no doubt. Of course, buddha nature doesn't depend on whether you recognize it or not—it is always buddha nature. Whether you recognize your own true nature or not just depends on your wisdom, or lack of it. You might fail to recognize your buddha nature because you are distracted by this samsaric life with its constant ups and downs, and you don't see things the way you are supposed to see them.

RECOGNIZING YOUR TRUE NATURE

Buddhism has a lot of labels. We talk about enlightenment, buddha nature, buddha—but what is a buddha? It's very simple: a buddha is someone who has achieved everlasting happiness, a peace that remains forever. This happiness is not something we need to believe in or to become; everyone already has it. The labels don't mean we need to become someone else; we don't need to create more labels. We have enough already. You have nondual pure awareness, or *rigpa* in Tibetan. We all have it. We call it the true nature of mind. That is buddha, and it's perfect.

This means you are already enlightened. Do you need to get enlightened again? No! You are enlightened already, and you don't need to make it better. It's already the best and has been from the beginning. There is no time in any case, so you never become worse, you never become better, your enlightened nature never changes. It's permanently pure and excellent. Dzogchen says you don't need to become someone. Trying to do that is fake anyway; you just need to recognize who you are. That is the ultimate experience.

We can keep on intellectually researching and looking outside of ourselves for some ultimate experience, but we will never be satisfied. There is no history of the mind becoming satisfied by research or by finding something. That's why we can keep on searching for years. We will never get the answer because real answers can't be found by mind. Only when mind rests can you get the answer. That's why trying to look for answers is an impossible pursuit. We just need to rest the mind.

Buddhism doesn't have a religious purpose. It's not about creating a new idea or giving you something to worship or follow. Its purpose is to explain the way things are. There is no need to change, we just need to recognize. We don't have to work hard to change anything, not at all. We are trying to discover our true nature, which is the peace that is already within us. We just need to discover that. This is not something we'll find somewhere else. We don't need to chase something or someone to get it; we don't need to make it happen, it is already within us.

Buddha nature is the great potential within every sentient being. We all have buddha nature, the wisdom that is born with us, has been with us all the time, and traveled with us from the beginning—we just have never recognized it. This is not something to believe in, nor do you need to create something to believe. Not at all. We just need to recognize, just as it is. That's what we call Dzogchen. We are not trying to worship something. We are talking about the mind. No matter your color, your culture, or your nationality, no matter what you believe or don't believe, you have a mind—and for as long as mind is there with you, you need to know how to free it from stress and suffering. You need to know how you can free yourself so that peace remains forever.

CHAPTER 2

Mind

> We are one hundred percent influenced by our
> intellectual mind. It is always saying, "Oh, you are
> not good enough, you have a problem."

TWO QUALITIES OF MIND

FROM THE DZOGCHEN point of view, mind has two qualities: one quality is very calm and peaceful, and the other is a bit chaotic. That second quality of mind is a little tricky; there is no stability and it can be quite crazy. One moment we can be really inspired and motivated to do good things, then suddenly the mind can switch and drive us in a completely negative direction. It is not that mind means to do this, it's just the relative nature of mind is tricky this way. It's always likely to be conflicted, to change, to go up and down and destabilize us. That's the job of the mind, it's supposed to do that. We are not meant to get surprised by this, because it's the mind's duty to behave this way. But we don't recognize that and instead ask, "Why is this happening to me?" But it is not you, it's your mind.

We are not judging mind as wrong, but it's important to understand that one part of mind is very sensitive and emotional. It's full of fear, doubt, and anxiety, things that we have created, and we live within that. There is nothing wrong with this; it's what Buddhism calls *samsara*. It's so important to look at your mind. What type of mind do you have at this moment? What state of mind are you in? Is it calm and peaceful or is it very disturbed? Is it distracted, happy, sad, or just so-so? Does it affect your life or not?

There are two ways to recognize mind. Firstly, if we recognize our way of life as difficult, chaotic, and inconvenient, but we can handle it, then mind won't bother us. For the moment, though, we can't handle it. The second way to recognize the mind is by cultivating a combination of wisdom and concentration so that we can handle it. Everyone has wisdom—we don't need to create or develop it—but that wisdom cannot lead us because we lack concentration. We are not allowing space for wisdom. We are keeping the mind busy with distractions and don't have the space to settle all these crazy thoughts.

MONKEY MIND

It's important to understand that we all have this distracted mind and mind is not easy. One mind isn't easy, two minds together are even harder, three are a complete headache. We are always blaming the world, blaming the system, blaming other people, but our problems have nothing to do with other people or the world; it is all to do with our mind. We try all sorts of things to find happiness. We look for joy and peace through fashion, social media, television, and so on, but nothing we discover really delivers happiness. It is a failure.

When we talk about mind in Buddhism, we introduce the idea that mind is like a monkey in a house with five windows. A single monkey is jumping around inside the house and looking through these five windows. From the outside, it looks like there are five monkeys. If someone were watching they would say, "Oh, there are five monkeys in that house, because I've seen one in that window and one in that," and so on. The rumors are already starting: "There are five monkeys in the house, did you know that?" The neighbors start this rumor, but the reality is that there is only one monkey, it's just visiting different windows. That's why we say the monkey is very cheeky, it doesn't stay in one place but keeps on running around. In the same way, our mind is jumping about between our five senses: going from the ears to the eyes, from the eyes to the tongue, from the tongue to the nostrils, from the nostrils to tactile feelings. We are never calm and stable.

We all have this mind, and when it's not resting, we are exactly like that monkey. The five senses are our different accesses, or screens, into the mind. Computers have Windows as an operating system, but we have the windows of the eyes, ears, nostrils, taste buds, and tactile sense. Mind is operating the functions of the relative world by looking at objects through each window—by seeing, hearing, smelling, tasting, and touching—but there is just one mind.

We talk a lot about mind, especially our intellectual mind that is always distracted. We are one hundred percent influenced by our intellectual mind. It's always saying, "Oh, you're not good enough. You have a problem." The intellectual mind always discourages us rather than giving us encouragement. Sometimes it might give you a small encouragement to catch you, but then it will pull you in the other direction. There is nothing necessarily wrong with the intellectual mind, but it can drive you crazy if you follow it too much. We need to learn about this intelligence. It wants to influence your decisions through the senses. Everything is reported back to this intelligence, which then says, "Yes, I like this," or "No, I don't like that." It makes a report and it influences the mind. "You will like this, but you aren't supposed to like that."

This so-called intelligent mind is based on ignorance. That's just how it is; our ignorance is leading us, not our wisdom. We have a bit of trouble telling the difference sometimes. We think, "Oh, that's not ignorance; it's something else, because I'm very clever." This is not clever; it's what we call "intelligence," and it creates all the shapes, colors, smells, tastes, feelings of our tangible experiences. It creates everything, and because it is the source of everything, it will tell us, "That's how it is." We develop all our experiences through this display of the intellectual mind. It's almost like an app developed by mind. We download this app into our system and then experience its function. You need to understand that.

Follow Your Wisdom

We need to understand the difference between mind and wisdom, or the mind and the heart. The heart is closer to wisdom. In spiritual terminology it is called "wisdom," but *heart* is the term we use in common language because everyone knows what *heart* means. Wisdom will naturally guide you once the mind is resting, but if the mind isn't resting, wisdom cannot guide you because you are not giving it the space and time it needs.

We try to follow the heart, to create space for the heart to lead, for wisdom to lead. Truly following your heart means letting go of your mind. Otherwise you cannot follow your heart, it's impossible. This is quite simple. Dzogchen is so simple. Some people think it's too simple, and that it cannot work. We are all intellectually educated, and our life has emphasized academic and other conceptual achievements, so we create more and more thoughts and never settle our minds. We keep creating complicated things and looking for complicated things, but we never settle our minds. Your best friend is your heart. If you can follow the heart, it will bring you to the right place. The mind will always try to start leading if it can. There are many good parts of the mind, it has many qualities, but it has many tricky parts, too. That's why we need to find balance.

There is only one moon above our world, but we can see moons reflected in all the lakes. There are thousands of lakes around the world, and a moon can be seen in each one. We separate ourselves by saying, "I am from this lake, you are from that lake, we are different." We try to separate ourselves from one another rather than merge into unity, but that separation creates fear. The tricky mind makes us afraid and tries to hold us there with thoughts of "Don't go there, it's the unknown, you are not safe." If you are afraid, your tricky mind is happy; if you are happy, your tricky mind is anxious, because you are doing something good. That's how the mind is. You need to change what you trust. Stop trusting your tricky mind and start trusting your heart. Your heart is in your chest, not in your head. If you follow your mind, forget about it—it will just go everywhere. If you follow your heart, everything will be great.

If we get rid of the monkey from the building and replace it with one big candle, how many lights will be seen through the windows? There will no longer seem to be five monkeys, there will be five lights. You can either have a monkey or a light, you have those two choices. It may look like there is a different candle in each of the five windows from the outside, but no, there is only one candle inside. That candle represents your inner wisdom. You can experience it through the five windows, and then you will see yourself and the world around you clearly. This is an example of how we can maintain the mind in meditation, so that it does not go to the left or right, to the future or the past, but instead remains focused on the present.

CHAPTER 3

Two Truths

You can't attain enlightenment until you let go of relative truth. You are not supposed to be attached to relative truth; you need to let it go and experience absolute truth.

RELATIVE AND ABSOLUTE TRUTH

BUDDHISM TEACHES two levels of truths: relative truth and absolute truth. If we don't understand the difference between these two truths, we will only see what is relatively true and believe that, and we will take it very seriously. Relative truth is karmic truth, the truth that says you will suffer if you harm others and you will be happy if you help others. There is no point in debating who is honest or lying, who is right or wrong, who is good or bad, who is helping or not, because that is all part of the karmic drama. On the absolute level, truth has nothing to do with these things; truth is beyond everything, it's beyond language, beyond action, beyond truth and lies, and beyond experience.

Positive karma, negative karma—everything is based on mind. When there is no mind, there is no karma, but as soon as mind is there, karma is there. If mind is at rest, karma is at rest. Dzogchen teachings say that good thoughts and bad thoughts are all just thoughts, so we don't encourage good thoughts or discourage bad thoughts. We need to get rid of both good and bad thoughts because they are all illusion. This is because relative truth is an illusion. We need to let go of relative truth so we can experience absolute truth. The absolute truth is that there is no relative truth. Everything that is part of relative truth is not real; these things are not true.

The Dzogchen tradition does not say there is no karma; it says that karma only functions when you follow your mind. This is referring to a different level of practice; the best way to get rid of thoughts is to rest the mind. When you can rest the mind, there will be no thoughts of the past, no thoughts of the future, and no thoughts of the present. When you can remain in that space, there are no consequences because consequences are part of karma. When mind stops acting and remains at rest, consequences no longer function. The more you rest the mind, the less you follow karmic law. You have that choice.

RELATIVE TRUTH

Buddhism has these two main subjects, relative truth and absolute truth. There are so many philosophical subjects within the relative. I studied them myself for thirty-five years. For those thirty-five years, I was looking for answers, but I never found them. I kept searching and searching, looking and looking. If you are reading this, you must be doing the same. You are looking for something—for some answers, for happiness, for peace. We try to find these things by applying different skills or looking in different places. What answer did I find after all those years of study? I found that I needed to stop searching! Once that happened, it was great; I felt relaxed. I had been continually stressing myself by searching and I didn't even know what I was looking for. We are all looking for something, but we need to have wisdom to know what we are looking for.

What is truth, really? You might say, "I heard someone tell a lie," but then you have an immediate problem, because anything that starts with "I" is ultimately untrue. For example, the Buddha told a disciple who was looking for happiness that you first need to give up saying "I want." In this case, the "I" is the ego and "want" is attachment. You can have happiness all the time if you drop "I" and "want." This "I want" belongs to the relative truth—and we like to make such a big deal out of relative truth.

We do need to make relative distinctions about what is true and what is right, but those distinctions are only ever true on the relative level. We can debate all we want about these distinctions, but they will never be ultimately true. They are only fake distinctions, so why do we make such a big deal of them? I'm not encouraging you to do anything wrong—not at all!—but sometimes we get so stuck and attached to relative truth and make too big a deal of it. Hinayana and Mahayana followers can become so attached to relative truth that it becomes hard for them to reach enlightenment. You can't attain enlightenment until you let go of relative truth. You are not supposed to be attached to relative truth; you need to let it go and experience absolute truth.

Hinayana and Mahayana schools talk about attachment in terms of specific categories, where things such as desire are bad and other things are beneficial. In the Dzogchen tradition, we do not talk about letting go of attachment to desire, we talk about letting go of attachment to all phenomena. This means letting go of your attachment to your own version of what is true. We are all attached to our own relative truths. You must let go of this attachment to relative truth because relative truth is not how things really are. Relative truth is full of fake stories and people who believe these fake stories. Social media is full of them, and people get sucked into that relative world.

When you let go of relative truth, you will recognize its unreality. That unreality is the absolute truth. For example, we may ask, "Is a red rose red?" Some people say, "Are you mad? Everyone can see the red rose is red." Other people say, "The rose is ultimately not there, so how can it be red?" There is no basis for the rose to be there. The rose is there only because the "I" is there to experience it. If the "I" is not there, the rose is not there. If the "I" is not there, the sky is not there; death is not there. So "I" and "want" is our big problem. We must let go of this "I" and "want," but it's very difficult to let them go because we say this all the time. That's just how we are.

It's always my way or no way. That's the samsaric drama. It's so important to understand this view of relative truth, because then you will see whether something is real or unreal, positive or negative, medicine or poison, and you will stop clinging to it. We have created all these things. That's the way we are.

There is a story about His Holiness Dudjom Rinpoche, Jigdrel Yeshe Dorje, that illustrates this. Laypeople would visit his temple and recommend something to Dudjom Rinpoche, saying, "This is very good for you, it's so wonderful, it's great." Rinpoche would say, "Yes, that's wonderful, that's great." The next person would tell him about the exact same thing, "This is very bad for you, it's terrible, it's not real." Rinpoche would say, "Yes, that's terrible, it's not real." The more intellectual people around him started wondering what was going on. Greatly realized people don't have any attachment to views. They don't say, "This is my view, this is my judgment, these are my principles, these are my terms and conditions." There are no such conditions for them. Things flow by like ocean waves and don't give them stress. This doesn't mean they don't know right from wrong; they just don't challenge other people's views.

We need to stop wasting our time with the things that come from mind. Everything born from mind is called "thought" and is not at all helpful. Dzogchen teaches meditation by saying "let go"—it never teaches us to hold on to something. You need to just let thoughts go.

Absolute Truth

There are two types of knowledge we can have: relative knowledge and wisdom knowledge. Relative knowledge is understanding karmic cause and effect, but this is quite limited knowledge. Wisdom knowledge is beyond that; it's recognizing that you have nothing to do with cause and effect, because cause and effect depend on the mind being distracted. As soon as the mind remains completely at rest, there is no karma, there is no cause and effect. Dzogchen meditation involves learning to stop following these thoughts. The more you rest the mind, the fewer thoughts you have, and the easier wisdom can come. The power of that wisdom is incredible.

The way we see things is not the same as the way they really exist. We believe things are the way we see them; we assume they must be like that because we see them like that. Like a mirage or an echo, they seem to be there, but they are not. That is our biggest challenge. We need to stop seeing things through our beliefs and start to see it as it is. We interact through our senses and interpret those interactions through our mind. Without the five senses, our minds would have no idea of the world. The senses make things real for us. Mind says, "My eye can see it, so that's how it is." But who can prove that what your eyes see is ultimately true? Nobody has proved that yet.

Dzogchen teachings say that what we see through our eyes is an illusion. We believe it is true because we see it—that sight is the evidence the senses report back to the mind. But remember, mind is like a monkey in a small room with five windows. We normally forget this and just follow this crazy mind, believing everything it says. We completely rely on it, and it keeps pulling us into that relative system. We are pulled completely into it and have no control. Absolute truth is not made-up truth. It's how things have always been. It's the genuine truth, but it is beyond explanation.

CHAPTER 4

The Dzogchen View

In Dzogchen, there is no relative view. The absolute
view is also unnecessary because everything
is absolute in Dzogchen.

The Importance of the View

THE DZOGCHEN PATH consists of view, meditation, and action (in
Tibetan, *tawa*, *gompa*, and *chopa*). The most important of these is
view, and here we can have either the right view or the wrong view. We
will have either right conduct or wrong conduct, right habit or wrong
habit, depending on our view. Everybody has a view, there's no doubt
about this. Most people believe what they see, hear, smell, taste, touch,
and think. All of that constitutes a view, but if you don't have the right
view, you will work too hard for enlightenment and be on the wrong
path. Whether you are on the right path or a wrong path depends on
your view.

We begin with the right view, and then we train in meditation. The
right view is like Mount Everest, because the bigger the mountain,
the more majestic, stable, and powerful the view. Meditation is like
the ocean, which is vast and deep. When you have right view and right
meditation, you will have right action, because nonduality will come by
itself. That's why we need to follow the order of view, meditation, and
action.

Having the relative view of the Mahayana path is like having a flashlight to light your way through the darkness at night. Wherever you shine your flashlight, you can see. The Dzogchen view is like the sunshine. You don't need the flashlight to help your vision or to chase after whatever you are looking for by shining a light around—you can see everything, because you can see the world with a different view during daylight. You can also take the flashlight journey to enlightenment, but you won't know what is in front of you or what is behind you.

It is common for us to have one view when we are meditating and another view when we are not meditating. When we are not meditating, we see, hear, smell, taste, and touch everything, and we have a lot of thoughts about them. When we meditate, that almost disappears, and we are quite peaceful for a moment. Meditation can help with calming the mind; it makes a difference, but having the right view is important. Having the right view will make our meditation really come alive.

It's difficult for us to stop believing in relative truth. We are born into it; it is like being stuck in a muddy pond and it's difficult to get out. We try many ways to get ourselves free, but what we most need is right view and meditation. Meditation is the training, but we need to begin with the right view. We need to believe absolute truth rather than relative truth. If you want to have a good life, you need right view and meditation. Your view is a way of life, it is something you develop into your system, into your body and your brain. Your view is about both the absolute view and the relative view because both views operate that system of body and brain. A one-year-old child sees everything with an open mind because their system is still pure, but later, when the child grows, they develop a view, and that view changes their system. This doesn't mean you can't do certain things. Being in the business world might make some things impossible, but the spiritual world is not like that—the spiritual world makes everything possible. You can do anything. That's the great thing, everything is possible.

Wrong View

What is it about the business world that restricts things? It has so much fear and wrong view. This lack of view leads to wrong meditation and wrong action. It makes everything so stressful that everyone panics, everyone has anxiety, fear, and worry. People think these things are normal and good, but this is not the right way to live. Sometimes we say, "Oh, my life is so stressful, I'm unhappy, I'm anxious." This is the result of having wrong view.

The difference between Dzogchen and other Buddhist schools is the other schools will have you believe that you are not already a good student, and you must become good. This is not the Dzogchen view. Dzogchen teachings say you have been a good student from the beginning, you just need to recognize it. That's it! Once you have that recognition, it doesn't matter what comes into your life—death, sickness, suffering, happiness, success—nothing will bother you, you will have gone beyond all that. There is no fear of death, no fear of change. Every moment is fun, every moment is joyful, every moment is peaceful. Imagine, that could be how you experience the world.

People say, "That's too difficult; that teaching is so deep, we will have to study for thirty years to get it." That is rubbish, I'm sorry to say. It's so simple, but we think it is difficult because the mind is so tricky. Your mind tells you that you cannot do it, but you *can* do it! You have got it. You don't even need to look for it, it's right there with you. People think that practicing Dharma is more difficult than samsaric life, but it is not. Practicing Dharma is actually easier than practicing samsara. We spend so many years studying Buddhism, but we don't gain anything. Dharma is not something to learn, it is something to recognize. You go beyond the learning. You just need to know it is there, and then you need to recognize it.

We need to develop our view to increase our understanding so we can realize and recognize. The moment you recognize, you unknot this samsaric net. For the moment, we are like fish caught in that net. Resting the mind helps us get the right view. This is not to say that resting the mind *is* the view, but resting the mind helps to lessen the thoughts that come up during that moment, and having fewer thoughts will help you get closer to right view.

Of course, you also need to manage your life. You can't just say, "Oh, whatever happens, happens." You still need to run your business, feed your kids, maintain your job, run your house, and pay the bills. Just saying "rest the mind" will not work—how does that help you to deal with the demands in your life? Having the right view can help you enjoy your life more. Meditation is a practice; it's a training. Whatever job you have, you need to prepare for it; first you study and study, then you train and train, and then you get the job. Meditation is also a training where you learn how to deal with things. Training is very important for everything in life.

Karma is another issue that is a big problem. We must all follow karma. We follow karma because we believe in it. We believe that if we sow a corn seed, a corn plant will grow. We believe that if we help someone, we create good karma, and if we harm someone, we create suffering. That is how karma works, but it's also a very complicated matter. Karma is so complicated—my goodness, there are millions of details! You must do this, you must not do that, you must have the right thoughts. But how can you control your thoughts? That's impossible. What *is* possible, however, is to just rest the mind and have the Dzogchen view. Then you won't need to worry about these millions of thoughts anymore. Dzogchen is beyond karma.

RIGHT VIEW

When we examine mind and ask ourselves, "What is mind?" we can see that mind is a kind of awareness. However, it is not pure awareness. There are two types of awareness: one is a pure awareness and one is a more regular kind of awareness. We believe in birth, sickness, and death, and we fixate on the things that we see, believe, and experience. This is a kind of awareness, but it's not pure awareness. We need to examine our view to analyze our mind so we see how preoccupied we are with this very active intellectual awareness. However, it's difficult to let go of that preoccupation because we are so engaged with our fixations. We find it hard to let them go. Sometimes people say, "No! I can't let that go, it's real for me! I can see it, I can smell it, I can feel it." That is the issue.

The Dzogchen teachings say we all have *rigpa*, our nondual pure awareness. They also talk about a mindful awareness, which is explained in a different way. With our mindful awareness, we can remember, we can think, and we can reflect, because on this level of awareness there is something to reflect upon. We can use this mindful awareness to recognize that we are agitated and need to be calm. In nondual pure awareness, however, there is nothing to reflect on, no one to reflect, and nowhere to reflect it. In Dzogchen, there is no relative view. To counter it with an absolute view is also unnecessary because everything is absolute in Dzogchen.

To have right view, you must examine your mind. Where has mind come from? Where does mind go? Where does it stay? You cannot find the mind because mind never goes anywhere, it never comes from anywhere, and it never stays anywhere. You cannot find it when you look, but if you don't examine it, mind pops up. That's the way it is. When you do this kind of examination, you may think you are playing hide-and-seek. The mind is hiding, and you are searching for it, but in truth there is nothing to search for and you are not going to find anything. We just believe that something or someone is hiding. We can spend a lot of time searching for the mind even though there is nothing to be found. We need to search for it though, because we believe it is there. That is the first stage of the view.

When you search for mind, you are looking for something that's impossible to find. Why have you spent five or ten or forty years doing that? There's no need to do that. What should you look for? The realization that you won't find mind whether you search for it or not, because there is nowhere for it to come from, nowhere for it to stay, and nowhere for it to go. When you don't examine mind, it is there. When you do examine mind, it dissolves. This is how mind is set up. How crazy is that? We believe in something that's not there; we rely on something that's impossible. We rely on something intangible, something we cannot see and cannot touch, but we still believe it exists. That's why we need to follow that process. This is a very serious matter, and this is why the Dzogchen teachings are always talking about mind. We are not making judgments about mind, saying it's good or bad; we are saying that mind is interesting. One part of it is very calm and peaceful and another part of it is totally unreliable.

CHAPTER 5

Stages of the View

*What you see when you look from your relative
eyes is different from what you see when you rest the
mind and see through your wisdom eye. It is a
different view, a different way of seeing.*

SEEING AND BELIEVING

THERE ARE three stages of the Dzogchen view: the relative view, the meditation view, and the absolute view. We can't mix these three together for the moment, because we are all quite different. The relative view is produced by what you see, hear, smell, taste, and touch through your senses, and you believe your view of these things. You have another view when you meditate. This view is still about what you experience through the senses, only now you don't believe what you see—you see it, but you don't believe it. The absolute view goes a step further because now you don't see it and you don't believe it. There are these three stages within the Dzogchen view. They are quite practical categories.

When you don't meditate and just live a normal life, you hear people talking and gossiping and creating dramas and politics. You are affected by this, you get distracted, you are happy or sad, everything is happening—and it is fine. It is like when you watch the news: one day there is drama about something, but two days later it has changed. This is our everyday relative view. There is nothing wrong with this view, but it is a view.

When you calm your mind in meditation, you can still see everything, but you no longer believe it, because you can see that everything is an illusion. You can still see it all, but you don't believe it. Then you can almost see things as a movie, a Hollywood movie, a Bollywood movie, your own mind movie. There are incredible movies going on in our minds all the time. Just as we need to recognize these movies as fake stories based on illusion, we need to recognize how many thoughts come and go, how many fake stories we entertain while imagining them to have some reality of their own.

The absolute view sees everything as empty. Not empty like a shopping bag is empty but empty of reality, because there is nothing, container or contained, to be empty. We don't need to make something empty, it's already empty. This is the same as saying we don't need to make it better, it's already the best. We don't need to change; we are already perfect. We don't need to worry about dying; we were never born and we never die, nothing ever changes. That is excellent. That is the right view. That is the absolute view.

These three views are illustrated by a story of an Indian magician. The magician creates a magic show where he uses a potion to conjure lions out of sticks and stones. The audience is affected by the potion, so everyone sees the lions and believes they are real. The magician also sees the lions, but he doesn't believe they are real. A passerby, unaffected by the potion, doesn't see anything but the magician moving sticks and stones around. We might get to the stage where we see things but don't believe them to be real, like the magician. We can also get to the stage where we don't even see things as real anymore, much like the passerby. Meditation can help us get to that stage and break the illusion. We must have right view to see things differently. It doesn't matter if you see it all as an illusion or not, the really important step is to stop believing it. That is yet another view. Maybe you don't believe it, and maybe you don't see it either. We only see what we believe to be there, so if we don't believe in this illusion, we may soon stop seeing it, too. We must learn to see it as it is instead of believing the magic show of samsara.

In the relative view, the first thing you need to understand is the cause and effect of karma. We say, "This produces bad karma, so don't do it; this creates good karma, so do it." At least with this approach you are doing something good. In the meditation view, you start to see how strongly illusion affects you and stop believing what you see. In the absolute view, awareness is called "nondual pure awareness" because there is nothing to believe, nothing to worry about—you have gone beyond any such duality. In this absolute view, you recognize that everything you experience or believe is an illusion. Not recognizing who you are is the root of that illusion. You cut the root of illusion when you recognize who you are. The problem is that you never go there.

RELATIVE VIEW

The relative view is important for understanding karmic structure. We need to know that karma is a law. We need to study the law of cause and effect, understand what does what and how things happen. Within the relative view, however, people are confused and have the wrong view. They don't see the cause of suffering and instead keep making the same mistakes. When people enter the spiritual path, they say, "Now I understand why I'm suffering; I'm creating my own suffering." That is the realization of relative truth, and it leads to the right view.

Everything we do should be done with right view. Anything that happens in samsara can make trouble for us, but we have this common-sense wisdom that can find the right view and that view can transform our problems into something we enjoy. When you have right view, your path will be the right path. That is the logic of Buddhism. We live in a very chaotic world; we're all in a very tough situation. People lack wisdom and they lack common sense. But if we have right view, we can live with that; the chaos won't bother us and we can challenge it.

We must understand samsara on the relative level. We live in samsara, we experience it through our five senses, and we endure suffering, happiness, sadness, birth, and death. On the relative level, all these things exist. But on the absolute level, those things do not exist, they are not happening; we go beyond it. We experience it just the way it is. The way it is, is different from the way we see it. When you look in the rearview mirror of your car, what you see there is not the same as what you see if you look directly behind you.

WISDOM VIEW

In the beginning, after we have developed right view, we then develop absolute view. Having right view can help you get the absolute view. The absolute view is neither right view nor wrong view—it's beyond both right and wrong. The simplest way to understand right view is to know that if something comes from your heart, it's the right view, and if it comes from your mind, it could be the wrong view. Anything from mind isn't genuine because it comes with expectations. The absolute view is pure, genuine, and without expectation.

What you see when you look from your relative eyes is different from what you see when you rest the mind and see through your wisdom eye. It is a different view, a different way of seeing. When you perceive the world with your wisdom eye, you have the wisdom view: your eyes become wisdom eyes, your ears become wisdom ears, your nose becomes a wisdom nose. You see things differently and you hear things differently. What's the difference? Whether something is good or bad, it doesn't affect you. It's like a one-year-old child going to the supermarket. They see everything but nothing bothers them. Then after three or four years they know, "This is ice cream, this is chocolate," and they get distracted. When you see things from the wisdom point of view, everything has one taste.

With the wisdom view, whatever you see is different; it's so inspiring, so relaxed and calm. Nothing ever changes you because you have completely conquered all emotion, feeling, and thought. The mind is no longer leading you. We have been under the control of our minds for so long. That's why we are completely stressed now. We burn out when we work too hard, but mind is always telling us, "You must do this, you must do that, you are not good enough, blah blah blah . . ." It's too much.

You need to stop that and start saying, "I'm not going to be a slave to mind anymore. I'm the boss!"

The Dzogchen view is the highest view, the view from the top of the mountain. When you have this absolute view, relative structures won't bother you. You are caught in a net, but you can cut the influence of the intellectual mind and free yourself from samsaric drama. We need to build a platform that will hold the view. That's why we meditate. Dzogchen is not intellectual. It is beyond logic, and we must break down that wall of the intellect and go to the other side. You'll find it very interesting when you apply the view of Dzogchen. You rest the mind, and then you listen, you think, you visualize, you talk to people—and it's different, it's completely transformed. You aren't reacting anymore, so life is very peaceful. Everything has become still and strong and clear, and nothing bothers you. That is the significance of the view.

CHAPTER 6

Beyond Time

When you rest the mind there is no time, but we
have created this illusion of the three times and we follow
this illusion. If time were to rest, nothing would bother us.

THE CONCEPT OF TIME

TIME IS an important subject in Dzogchen. Within relative truth, we have the three times—past, present and future—and we follow them accordingly. That's how we operate on the relative level. On the level of absolute truth within Dzogchen, there is only one time. We call this the fourth time or permanent time, because past, present, and future become one. It isn't really time, however; we just give it that label. This fourth "time" is not the kind of time that changes. It is beyond time.

The concept of time is interesting. The Western world is quite chaotic because it keeps chasing time. Everyone is driven nuts by the intense pressures of time. We create a schedule, and then we can't follow it, so we feel stressed when we don't reach our goals. When we are late for an appointment due to a traffic jam, late for work or for a job interview, for shopping, school, or meeting friends for coffee, everybody else shows their mood and complains, "Why are you late?" That is all because of time. Our time is very limited, and we are stuck with that. We are busy and tired, and we have no time, even though time is not there. We say, "Oh, this schedule! I must finish this, I must do that!"

We have a lot of experiences due to the passing of time: depression, stress, burnout, happiness, sadness. And then we must do everything on time, which creates a lot of pressure, and if we can't complete a task, we panic and create more stress. If you can't finish something on time, that's fine, it's not a disaster. You tried your best and it didn't work out, so accept it. That is an interesting challenge for all of us.

THE THREE TIMES

Time is an illusion. Who created it? Our mind created it. We created time and we follow time, but there is no such thing as time. We make it up through our ideas of past, present, and future. When you rest the mind there is no time, but we have created this illusion of the three times and we follow this illusion. If time were to rest, nothing would bother us. That's why the Dzogchen view understands the three times as relative. "Relative" means we keep on chasing past, present, and future and being distracted by them. But are they really of benefit to us or do they just give us more trouble? On the relative level, our happiness is only short term. We work hard to maintain our pleasure, but pleasure is very fleeting. It is impermanent and it keeps on changing. Change is the nature of samsara. That's why, to understand the relative view, it's important to introduce the three times, but we must know that according to the absolute view, there is only permanent time.

The past is finished, yesterday is complete. We can't go back to yesterday and we can't go forward to tomorrow either, because it is still today. That's what we call the "relative function." Mind creates movement and mind creates time. We are always busy because we live in time. The mind is very clever, it hides backstage from this powerful production. Dzogchen is like a science of the mind that helps us understand how mind creates the relative system. We can improve our lives based on that understanding, which is why it's important to understand the three times from the relative perspective.

When we remain in meditation and experience calm, we feel very peaceful, a complete pause, because we live in samsaric time. We experience karma because karma is dependent upon time. We experience sickness, old age, death, suffering, happiness, sadness, and so on because of time. Time is what allows us to experience these things. If time didn't change, none of these things could happen; we would just remain calm and peaceful because there would be nothing to experience. Everything else is just a dream. Whether it's a good dream or a bad dream, it's still only a dream. It ceases to be real when you wake up.

Time is moving quickly now; it seems we're always short on time. As adults, we feel challenged to make time last longer or to somehow make time become permanent. When I was a child, the time from morning to lunch took so long. I would ask myself, "When am I ever going to eat lunch?" These days, as soon as breakfast is finished, it seems like it's already time for dinner, the day goes so quickly. Is time getting shorter? Maybe. We don't know. Maybe it's just that we are too busy and too distracted to notice time passing and we can't enjoy it.

THE FOURTH TIME

With Dzogchen, we are introducing a fourth time: permanent time. This may be a new concept for you, as it is outside the familiar structure of past, present, and future. We have emotions and stresses because time passes. Our experiences never last, they keep on changing. The time we call the fourth time is "permanent time." It is very stable; it is continuous and unchanging. That means you can remain in peace continually because this peace is not going to change.

When you really see that the three times are fabrications, time stands still. In your normal state, time is still playing in your mind; you are still watching, eating, thinking. Those thoughts are all present. But in the fourth time, there are no thoughts. It's completely silent, completely clear, very pleasant and peaceful. Past thoughts are gone, future thoughts stop coming, and present thoughts immediately dissolve. When you get rid of the three times, there is a time called "no time." That is another label for it. We need these labels to explain Buddhism through human communication. This time of no time is the fourth time.

All thoughts belong to the three times. So where are those thoughts when the three times are gone? They completely disappear when time becomes permanent. This is the absolute unity, permanent time, or what we can also call absolute time. There is nowhere for thoughts to arise. Where is the stress? Where is the fear? Where is the worry? The space for all that is gone. As we say in Dzogchen, "The three times become one time."

The three times are changeable, but they become timeless when they are reduced to one time, because there are no changes in the time of no time. Time remains forever. It becomes permanent time or absolute time. Seeing that is what we call "recognizing your true nature." In that moment, you realize that time is completely at rest, and when time is at rest, you experience rigpa, your nondual pure awareness. It's just there. You don't need to search for it. You will just experience it immediately, on the spot.

There is no past, no future, no present, no change; everything becomes the fourth time. What name can we give "time" then? We can't call it the present, we can't call it the past, we can't call it the future, so we call it "timeless time." That is the miracle. We can remain very peacefully in timeless time because it doesn't keep changing. The past is finished, it is no more. The future has not yet come. We can experience the present moment, but it's better not to get distracted by it. When we talk about time from the absolute point of view, we are talking about timeless time, where we can remain in peace and happiness forever.

BREAKING THE HABIT OF TIME

Time is our biggest habit. We believe time exists, so we live in time. Time is passing; we are in the present, but tomorrow is coming, and today will become the past. We have so many past, present, and future activities. We believe in all of them because the mind makes us believe it. There is no reason to believe it, but mind makes us believe it anyway. The mind has so many thoughts, and Dzogchen practice is about trying to cut that chain of thought. We do this by trying to break the habit of our belief in time.

The experience of permanent time might seem quite boring. We love to be constantly active, and if we don't keep busy, we don't feel alive. In some ways, human life requires us to be active and productive, but will that bring more peace and happiness or will it bring more headaches? It's amazing that we don't want to stay in this timeless time. We are habituated to follow past, present, and future because we love these moments of change. We like to move and we are influenced by our old habits, we love things to keep changing. Sometimes, when change comes, you feel it as a kind of suffering—but it's just change. Change is suffering, change is the obstacle, change is the problem.

People also don't want to experience permanent time because they are afraid of it. In Tibetan, we have an expression for this: "the fear of the rabbit." A rabbit is afraid the sky is going to fall. We likewise worry that something will go wrong. But nothing will go wrong—the sky is not going to fall. It's safer to let the three times remain in oneness than to follow them in fear. We have so much fear of something going wrong and so we panic. We need to realize that time is an illusion. The three times are just a distraction. Every single mind exists within the three times, within the past, present, and future, and every single thought belongs within them. A buddha is beyond the three times.

The three times are simply objects of illusion. There is no past, there is no present, and there is no future. This is not to say that time is no longer there; it means that time was never there to begin with. We just believe that time is there. We think, "If time doesn't exist, how could my physical form be here?" Our physical form and our intellectual mind all come from time. We were born, we remain for a while, and then we die. We need the three times for that. If the three times are no more, there is nowhere to be born, nowhere to stay, and nowhere to go.

Time can be permanent, but only because it never changes. When you calm the mind in meditation, there are brief moments of real silence and peace without change, which is an example of living in timeless time, of going beyond time. Change only happens in samsaric time. That is where we suffer, where we are stressed by the past, where we worry about the future, and where we struggle with the present. When time rests, we are still and calm.

CHAPTER 7

Direct Experience

The view of Dzogchen can only be experienced
through meditation. We cannot express it
or experience it through language.

MEDITATION

D ZOGCHEN IS very simple and practical. The result of Dzogchen practice is experienced on the spot, we are not saying it's going to happen sometime in the future. When you do it, you can experience it on the spot. However, you can only experience this result through your own meditation; it cannot be described or expressed through language. It is just like when you put chocolate on your tongue, you cannot express the taste of sweetness or replicate the experience through language. The taste of chocolate can only be experienced by the tongue. In the same way, the view of Dzogchen can only be experienced through meditation. We cannot express it or experience it through concepts.

We learn what is good and what is bad in an intellectual way. That is okay, but we need to know that all this analysis and judgment is a bit unnecessary. You must learn to focus in meditation—keeping your practice as simple as possible is best, so long as you just keep focusing. When you've focused the mind like this, then you can see what percentage of the time your mind goes to the past and what percentage of the time your mind goes to the future. It is interesting to see that. If you can minimize the time your mind goes to the past and future, you have already accomplished something, you are already at a good stage, you have already proven something. You have something to measure your progress by.

What type of mind do you have now? Is your mind more worried or stressed by the past or future? Some people are more preoccupied by the future, some people are more focused on the past, some might be equally in both, and some not swayed by either. It depends on your lifestyle. We try to meditate a little to benefit the mind and to benefit that monkey in the house, too. We do this because we want to learn how the monkey and the mind can become calm and peaceful. The reason to calm the mind is that as soon as the mind is peaceful, wisdom immediately arises, and then joy and genuine fun will pop up. We don't need intellectual fun. It's very important to keep space for the heart to lead, so we need to have a calm and peaceful mind. That is a requirement. The logic of these skills, these meditation methods and practices, is very important because they are how we can bring calm and peace to the mind.

In Dzogchen, we talk about the mind, nothing else—how to calm the mind, how to rest the mind. That is very important. Resting the mind is quite simple in Dzogchen, and I will explain that in the next section. We have a mind, and it is either functioning or resting; it has these two states. We call it "relative" when the mind is not resting, and we call it "absolute" when the mind is resting. It's that simple. If we want to reach the resting state, we need to learn to meditate. That is stage one. Meditation is not the destination; meditation is the path or vehicle that we use to reach our destination. Once you reach the destination, you don't need to meditate.

ONE TASTE

Shamatha is the form of resting meditation that leads to the extraordinary view, which comes in the moment that mind is calm and peaceful. You can get this extraordinary view by resting the mind. You don't need to look for it or to create it. Your mind will be very clear, not cloudy. Through this meditation, we try to give more space for the heart to lead.

Once your heart starts leading, you will have a different experience. If your mind leads, it drives you nuts; we all know that quite well. We are used to doing that a lot. I do the same thing. When I follow my mind, I can see that it's completely mad. Luckily, I can recognize that. But if I follow my mind, forget it. So I try to rest my mind again by telling myself how wonderful it is to have seen my own distraction.

You might think, "This is a Buddhist lama, he's got a lot of wisdom," but you should not judge like that. We are exactly alike, you and I. We are the same, there is no difference. What I learned from studying Buddhist philosophy and completing my advanced studies was nothing. I didn't get anything from it, sorry to say. The difference between that and what I learned through meditation is everything. I got all my realization from meditation. All my experience became one taste.

Until I experienced meditation, I didn't fathom "one taste," everything had a different taste for me. I was confused until my master taught me meditation and gave me an introduction to one taste; he told me it was the essence of the Buddha's teachings. Everything became oneness, a unity, one taste. There's no difference between samsara and nirvana, no right or wrong, no good or bad, no suffering and no happiness. This is important to understand. I'm like you, I studied philosophy for many years, searching for happiness, searching for answers. In the end, I couldn't find any and realized there was nothing to find. We keep searching for nothing and cannot find it. So don't waste your time searching, it is better to rest. I learned how to rest and that is more fun.

PART 2

Methods

CHAPTER 8

Mindfulness

Mindfulness is used to focus the mind. The mind usually
goes in all directions and we become giddy from spinning
and going everywhere. We end up like a motor that
has been revved too high and burns out.

FOUR FOUNDATIONS OF MINDFULNESS

THESE DAYS many people are writing books on mindfulness, but
it's not a new thing in Buddhism. Gautama Buddha taught the
four foundations of mindfulness over 2,500 years ago. These four foundations are a relative method for reducing stress. They are extremely
helpful techniques for calming the mind. The four foundations include
mindfulness of body, mindfulness of feelings, mindfulness of mind, and
mindfulness of dharmas. Mindfulness helps us balance different levels
of emotion, so it's important that body, feelings, mind, and actions are
aligned in what we call "the moment of being present together." Normally, your body is in one place, your feelings are elsewhere, and your
mind is thousands of miles away. You are not connected. Sometimes, we
disconnect from all four foundations, which is why we are a little confused. Your mind cannot see what you are doing because your body is
not in step with your thoughts, your thoughts are not in step with your
feelings, and your feelings are disconnected from your actions.

Mindfulness of body

Meditation, physical postures, sports, and yoga are all very helpful for your body. It's true that certain postures can help us reduce stress and balance our emotions, which is why yoga and mindfulness are excellent, sports are excellent, and, of course, shamatha meditation is also excellent. Mindfulness of body means that the physical posture we hold in meditation is very helpful for calming the body. In Dzogchen, we just leave the body as it is, let it be the way it is, keep it as it is. You don't need to convert or change anything. Just let the body relax how it is; don't try too hard. Simply allow your physical posture to rest comfortably.

Mindfulness of feelings

Mindfulness of feelings means we notice our feelings without following them. When a good feeling comes, you don't make a big deal of it, and when a bad feeling comes, you don't make a big deal of that, either. When you can do this, your meditation on the mindfulness of feelings is working. Normally, we tend to pick and choose our feelings: "I like the feeling of this, but I don't like the feeling of that; this harms me, that hurts me, I don't like it." You try to push it away. We call pushing our feelings away "blocking" them, but they only get worse when we block them. You should let your feelings come and let your feelings go, but don't follow them. For example, if you try to block fear when it comes, you will end up with more fear. It's better to let fear come without following it because then the fear will disappear without disturbing you. You will be like a highway hotel, where both positive and negative thoughts and feelings are like travelers that stay for a night and are gone the next day. When you stay in a highway hotel, you can book a room for the night, but you must leave the next day; your time is up, you can't stay forever. It's the same thing with thoughts and feelings. They just come and they go. You are like that hotel with different thoughts coming and going, different experiences coming and going.

Mindfulness of mind

The same approach is used for mindfulness of mind. All the thoughts that come—wild thoughts, positive thoughts, negative thoughts, complicated thoughts, jealous thoughts, kind thoughts, compassionate thoughts—are of no use because they are all equally thoughts. We must let thoughts go, let them rest. Mindfulness is used to focus the mind. The mind usually goes in all directions and we become giddy from spinning and going everywhere. We end up like a motor that has been revved too high and burns out. Once a motor burns, even a little bit, you need to repair the whole thing. You must maintain your car by changing the grease and oil and taking care not to run it too high. The car will be okay if you fix those things and run it properly. Your mind and body work together in the same way—we learn to focus and rest the mind to keep our body and mind in good health.

We get physically stressed because mind is clever and tricky and acts like a tyrant, leading us wherever it wants. That's why we must be careful. But we don't need to worry or panic about our minds, and think that the mind is doing something bad when this happens. People blame their problems on all kinds of things—thinking it must be the weather, it must be the country, it must be the food. Our problems have nothing to do with any of that. We need to be aware that all good and bad experiences come from our own mind and nowhere else.

If mind is there, problems will be there, even if we change everything else. If mind is not settled, our problems will not settle. If the mind can be calmed, our problems will resolve by themselves. It doesn't matter if you change the weather, change your country, or change your house, the most important thing you can do is change your mind. Sometimes we fix up our house and garden so that everything outside is very clean, but we need to clean our minds, too. If you don't clean your mind, there will still be a lot of rubbish inside. We need to have a clean mind and clean thoughts. Just like a computer, our hard drive gets full; it won't shut down, it won't open programs, it starts running slow. Our mind needs to be cleaned up, to have things deleted, to create space. We call that rubbish "the pollution of the mind." It's very important to detox from our unnecessary stress, thoughts, worries, and fears. We must get rid of that.

Mindfulness of dharma

There are two definitions of the Sanskrit term *dharma* (translated into Tibetan as *cho*). The philosophical meaning of the term is "spiritual teachings," which we call Dharma, with a capital *D*. The other meaning of dharma is "phenomena." In regard to one of the four foundations of mindfulness, the dharmas we are talking about here are all the phenomena that exist in the world. Everything good and bad is a dharma. For example, when you go to have lunch, every element is a dharma. What did you eat for lunch? Where did you sit? What did you talk about? Each of these experiences is a dharma.

Ultimately, mindfulness of dharmas means seeing everything as it is. There is nothing else to see. For the moment, we're not seeing things as they are—we are labeling, interpreting, and judging everything. We label things and then judge them, thinking, "I like this, I don't like that." We pick and choose. When we are caught up in the fixations of mind, we are not being mindful of dharmas. We fail to see everything as it is because we are confused and judgmental rather than mindful of the pure experience.

OBSTACLES TO MINDFULNESS

There are two main obstacles to these mindfulness meditations: laziness and restlessness. Laziness is very dangerous in meditation because it stops you accomplishing anything. Restlessness is a little dangerous because your mind becomes too wild and can't be calm and peaceful. If you are too lazy and do nothing, your meditation won't have any continuity. If you are restless, your mind will become panicky—going up and down, this way and that way—and you won't be able to calm it. It's like having a monkey in your room that is jumping everywhere. You need to find the balance that falls into the middle path: not too lazy, not too restless.

Both laziness and restlessness come and go. Your mind isn't necessarily always wild, and it isn't necessarily always lazy. From time to time you will think, "I'm tired, I'm not going to meditate." There is nothing wrong with feeling restless or lazy, but understand it's an obstacle that is not so good for your meditation practice. You don't need to push yourself too hard either, saying, "I don't want to be lazy; I don't like laziness." Just don't make too big a deal of it and it won't harm you. Our ability to deal with this progresses in stages. We take things very seriously in our practice at first, thinking everything either harms us or helps us. As we progress and stop taking things so seriously, they don't bother us and they leave us alone. In the end, whether something is there or not there doesn't matter to us or our ability to meditate.

When the mind becomes peaceful, we experience positive gains. Everything becomes quite clear; there is less confusion and less fear. The purpose of meditation is to give you freedom from your mind. Right now, you are like a captive to your tricky, intellectual mind; you do whatever mind tells you. Our minds are usually one hundred percent influenced by the five negative emotions: desire, jealousy, greed, pride, and ignorance. We have no freedom from them as long as we follow the mind. What we need is a freedom where all our emotions become balanced, where we can experience peace.

These emotions come from an imbalance in our view to begin with. You are either completely tired or you are overexcited, never calm; you are hot or cold, never warm. Hot is too hot and can burn you, while cold is too cold and can give you a chill. Warm is much better because it gives you continuity. Human beings can be quite sensitive and thin-skinned. We tell ourselves and others, "You can't say that; you can't do that; it's too much." We are so defensive about our body, feelings, and mind, which is why we need to learn to rest them. We need to stop taking everything too seriously. If something is wrong, whatever the situation, that's fine. This is not to say that you don't need to care about anything—altruism has nothing to do with it. We must have compassion and take responsibility for things. We just don't need to get too stressed about it.

For example, many Western people go to Asian countries to work for charities, but if they don't have a spiritual foundation and are weak and sensitive themselves, they just become stressed by charity work. They end up saying to me, "Oh my goodness, the need for this work is never going to end," and they become really depressed. I say to them, "That is not the way to think about this situation. Why are you depressed? You are taking everything too seriously." When you go to a country where everything is chaotic, you need to understand that nothing is perfect and that's okay. Even if things were perfect, it wouldn't be any better, because even perfection would not change things much. We have this habit of needing things to be perfect, to be in good order, because we think order is better. But that is just another view. It's better not to take things too seriously.

The purpose of mindfulness is twofold. The first is to learn to focus our attention on every detail so that we can recognize our body, feelings, phenomena, and mind. The second is to recognize our negative emotions rather than be driven by them. We are learning not to react to everyday life. When you can do this, your mind will become very powerful. It is powerful already, but it's only when your mind is balanced that you can recognize this power.

CHAPTER 9

Shamatha

A calm mind allows your great potential, your buddha
nature or pure awareness, to arise more often.

THE PRESENT MOMENT

W E NEED to practice meditation because it's not enough to have a view. If your destination is a mountain, it's not enough just to look at the mountain; you need to walk toward it, you need to start the journey there. Our journey starts with shamatha meditation. Shamatha is the method that brings about right view, because we have to calm the mind to experience that view. The relative method of shamatha reduces stress and confusion by focusing the mind so it can stay in the present moment. Our minds are completely busy with distractions so we never give space to wisdom, we never create the space necessary to settle all these crazy thoughts. We need to calm and pacify the mind by focusing it. A mind that is calm and peaceful is shamatha. This concentration helps the mind to become less stubborn and more pliable. We train this monkey mind of ours by calming it down and focusing our attention on the present.

Our minds are so distracted by the past and future, we never focus on the present. For example, say you leave the house to go shopping and you lock the front door, but you are not present in the moment you lock the door because you are distracted and your mind is already in the shopping center. On the way to the shopping center, you start to worry,

"Did I lock the door?" You keep stressing about it until you turn back and have to push and pull the door to check that it is locked. You don't feel comfortable until you go back and check it. You go on holiday for a week and constantly worry, "Did I lock the door? Did I close the windows? Did I switch off the gas? Did I lock the car?" We carry so much stress through simply not being present. Our physical body was there when we left the house, but our mind was not. That's called distraction. We create stress for a completely silly reason.

So what is the remedy? Concentrate more on what you are doing. When you are locking the door, just be in front of the door. Make sure you are there; as you lock the door, think, "Yes, I have locked the door." Then you can remember: I was there, I've seen it, I've got the key, I was standing in front of the door. Tick the box, have the mind register it in the logbook. Then, when you go shopping, you will be completely free of worry, you won't need to think back and wonder what you did. You can just enjoy shopping, your lunch, or whatever you are doing.

SHAMATHA WITH SUPPORT

When you practice shamatha, you focus your mind on an image or an object. Take the metaphor of a candle flame. If you place a candle before you when there is a slight draft in the room, it will flicker just a little. When there is no wind at all, the flame will be stable and the circle of light around it will be clear. When there is a breeze, the flame will be unstable, blowing to the left and right, and the light around it will be hazy. The candlelight stands for knowledge, but knowledge alone is not enough, we also need concentration. Concentration is an atmosphere without disturbance, where the flame doesn't get blown to the left or right. You can look at a candle and then visualize your mind as that candle. Is it stable or is it wavering? When the mind is stable, you can see and hear much better.

Focusing like this is very helpful. When you focus, your mind becomes stable for that moment, it's no longer going everywhere. This practice is just a beginning. It's not going to make huge changes in your life, only small changes, but at least your mind will be more stable. That on its own is already quite an improvement. Otherwise, the mind goes everywhere, it points our nose in every direction, so much so that we sometimes cannot handle it. We go to the future, we go to the past, we worry, we doubt, we panic. Our minds are sometimes in complete chaos.

There are different forms of shamatha meditation, in Tibetan called *ten che* and *ten me*, which mean "with support" and "without support." When you look at an object, you can see it very clearly; your eyes are open and looking at the object. In shamatha "with support," you look at an object of support and you observe it clearly for a few minutes. You have the complete picture. In the moment that you see the object, you don't look left or right, you just look directly at it. The object of support in shamatha can be further classified as an impure object or a pure object. An impure support is something like a plant, a pebble, a flower, or a piece of wood. You can put anything there in front of yourself to look at. It's called an "impure" object because it's an ordinary object, likely something from nature. A "pure" object would be an image of the Buddha, such as a statue or painting, or a stupa, or mala.

Shamatha with impure support

When you are beginning meditation, start with this simple shamatha practice. Place a potted plant on a table in front of you and concentrate on that. This is the first step to training for your mind. You want your mind to be able to concentrate, otherwise it will go to the future and the past, left and right, never staying centered. It is good to start by just focusing and concentrating on that plant. When your mind starts to stray, just gently bring it back to the plant in front of you. You don't need to worry about meditating on statues or religious objects if a plant can help you start to train your mind. When you focus on the object you will experience a moment of presence, a moment of space, freedom, calm, joy, and peace. Usually the mind just spins around, going to past worries or future worries, never settling, and just keeps churning out millions of thoughts.

Shamatha with pure support

After a while you can do the same meditation using a pure object, such as a picture of Guru Rinpoche, Buddha, Tara, Manjushri, or a deity of your choice. Place that in front of you and look at it very clearly. Look at the colors, the shape, the number of eyes, the number of arms, the decorations, and so on, so that you can visualize it clearly even when you are not looking directly at it. It might be easier to start with Shakyamuni Buddha or a deity with only two arms and one head. This tradition has buddhas with a thousand arms and a thousand eyes, and my goodness, you might get confused if you try to visualize that! It can take ages to get to the point where you can visualize all the details, so practice with a simple buddha, such as Guru Rinpoche or Tara, someone who looks like we do. Look at the picture or statue in front of you and see all aspects of its form clearly; take complete notice of it all.

SHAMATHA WITHOUT SUPPORT

Once you've gained some experience in shamatha with support, you can move on to doing the practice without support. Immediately after you have looked at an impure or pure object, close your eyes and visualize what you just saw in your mind. Imagine all the details exactly as you saw them. As you develop in this practice, it's important to close your eyes and be able to see the exact shape of the object in front of you, whatever it was—a plant, a stone, a statue, a painting—and recall the object in every detail. First you see the object clearly with your eyes open and then you recall every detail of the object with your eyes closed. Visualization is to see with your mind. You close your eyes and visualize the shapes and colors until you are seeing the exact same thing that you saw with your eyes open.

This may take some time to accomplish, so you need to train in it again and again. Keep on practicing by looking at the object and then closing your eyes and visualizing it. Then look at the object again, close your eyes, and visualize it, and so on. The object and your visualization of the object will become more and more alike until you can see an object clearly when your eyes are closed. We call this "training in visualization."

This training is quite a good one to start with when you are practicing shamatha without support. There's no need to do too much at the beginning; just focus on very simple things. Put something on your table, look at it, and concentrate on the details. Try to see it without allowing your thoughts to go to the past or the future, just be there for maybe five minutes, then close your eyes and visualize the same object in your mind. When you open your eyes again, just look at the object again for a while, then close your eyes and visualize it again in your mind.

When you meditate and look at an object with your eyes open, it's called "meditation with support," or *ten che*, and when you visualize an object with your eyes closed, it's called "meditation without support," or *ten me*. This system is a technique for training the mind. You are training your mind to be more focused, so that it has fewer distractions, less intellectual activity, and more heart. That is the training and the purpose of the training. This is a good method because it involves visualization and will prepare you for the development and dissolution stages of tantric practice, where precise visualization becomes very important. We need to begin the practice of visualization in this simple way to prepare ourselves for those further practices.

VISUALIZATION

We train in shamatha meditation stage by stage so that we can go deeper and deeper, and at the same time, higher and higher. When we come to Vajrayana training, shamatha involves visualizing mandalas emerging from seed syllables. That is a form of shamatha without support because the whole process takes place in your mind. Sometimes the seed syllable is a HUNG, sometimes a HRIH, sometimes something else. We visualize a single seed syllable—a primordial sound that embodies the essence of samsaric realms, buddha realms, and wisdom deities—and develop a whole mandala from that. We create the mandala from emptiness; we start by visualizing the seed syllable emerging from empty space and then visualize a whole mandala emerging out of that. At the conclusion of the visualization, we dissolve everything back into the seed syllable and then dissolve the syllable back into empty space.

A complete mandala can be almost as elaborate as a whole city. That's why we need training in visualization, to be able to see this level of detail in our mind. This is called *kyedzog Dzogchen*, a practice that includes *kyerim* (visualization) and *dzogrim* (dissolution). Kyedzog is a shamatha practice on the Vajrayana path where we train in calming the mind at a much deeper level.

Dzogchen is trying to introduce the idea that all of us, whether we practice visualization or not, are already a buddha. We try to feel we are a buddha by visualizing enlightened deities and gaining an experience of what that would be like, since we are naturally born a buddha anyway. We get as close as possible to the visualization so that we can really have an experience of being that deity. As human beings, our minds are naturally quite creative, and we imagine we are permanent somehow, so we need to dissolve the visualization of being a buddha back into emptiness, bringing us back into the level of our true nature. We always do visualization and dissolution practice together.

EXTRAORDINARY VIEW

Shamatha makes it possible to bring about the extraordinary view, or vipashyana, when your meditation progresses. *Vipashyana* is a Sanskrit term for the extraordinary view of clarity and insight. We have a strong yet mistaken picture of our status as a human being and we need to realize the falseness of thinking "I am here." When you examine it, that "I" cannot be found. We can build upon and support our shamatha with an analytical meditation that examines the "I" through certain questions, such as: Where is the I? Where does it come from? Where is it going? Where does it stay?

When you can calm your mind and maintain the continuity of that calm, you will get the extraordinary view of clarity, and once you become stabilized in shamatha, vipashyana will pop up naturally. Everything will be okay when that clarity is there, you will have the right view and choosing the right action will be easy. You will no longer be swayed by feelings of stress, anger, or jealousy. All those thoughts will still be there, but you find you no longer react to any of them. A mind that is calm and peaceful is a result of shamatha, and that calm gives rise to the experience of seeing things more clearly, which is vipashyana.

ABSOLUTE SHAMATHA

The purpose of shamatha is to recognize relative truth and then merge into absolute truth, which means we have both relative shamatha and absolute shamatha. Relative shamatha, which is what we have covered so far, is not Dzogchen meditation, but it will give your mind more space so that it becomes less stubborn and more pliable. When mind is more pliable and less stubborn, it is easier to practice Dzogchen meditation.

Dzogchen has two stages of shamatha. The first is to remain in the present moment without following thoughts about the past or the future, which is still a form of relative shamatha. The second is to rest the mind and not even remain in the present, which is absolute shamatha. Absolute shamatha is a Dzogchen practice in which we bring our minds to complete rest and all thought dissolves. Then we simply maintain the continuity of that dissolution.

We need to practice relative shamatha to learn to stop following thoughts about the past and thoughts about the future so that we can simply concentrate on the present moment. We practice the visualization and dissolution stage to reach absolute shamatha, because when you train the mind to visualize things, you start every visualization from empty space and dissolve it back into empty space. We then learn to go beyond time altogether and rest the mind without thought. Combining the practices of shamatha and analytical meditation will develop the view of clarity and insight. Vipashyana can also pop up naturally through absolute shamatha, because when all thoughts dissolve, the view will come up by itself.

TRAINING THE MIND

The aim of this book is to give you a general view of Dzogchen, and we have started by giving you an overview of the purpose of shamatha. We are looking at the relative purpose, the absolute purpose, and the benefits of shamatha. What can you gain and what are you looking for? The answer is everlasting happiness. Where do you start if you want to get there? You must start where you are.

If you have a piece of metal and give it to a swordsmith, they can make a sharp sword from it. The sword is already within the piece of metal, but you need the swordsmith to shape it and bring the sword out. Similarly, we need to apply the methods and skills that can turn our mind into a sword that can cut through our ignorance. That's why it's so important to continually train the mind, starting by sitting and meditating in front of a potted plant and staying with this practice until you gain the great state of visualization.

Shamatha is about bringing your concentration to the present and not following your thoughts. We concentrate on the same thing again and again and again, because repetition makes it part of our lives. We are not looking for answers or solutions anymore, we just repeat the practice over and over. This is how we train the wild mind. It's hard to direct a wild animal and it's hard to direct a wild mind, but if we give the monkey mind direction and calm it down, it will learn to follow a master rather than its own impulses.

A calm mind allows your great potential, your buddha nature or pure awareness, to arise more often. When you can recognize that potential you feel stronger, more confident, and more grounded, with less fear and doubt. That's the benefit of shamatha. When the mind is calm, peaceful, and settled, you can see things clearly, you have these incredible qualities. When the mind is agitated and unsettled, it becomes dangerous, because you can't see things clearly and your thoughts are nonstop. That is mostly how we live life on the samsaric level, the mundane level of business, politics, family, health, and relationships. We all argue and debate and it gets quite tiring. It's an endless cycle of "You're wrong, I'm right," until we are completely exhausted.

The purpose of relative shamatha is to break our habit of believing in this monkey mind by settling it down and bringing calm. Absolute shamatha is Dzogchen; it is only taught in Dzogchen. It's what we call "resting the mind" and is usually taught after the relative forms of shamatha have been stabilized. Ordinary teachings on shamatha stop at the relative stage and don't lead you to rest the mind in this way. In Dzogchen, we start with the practice of relative shamatha because you must first see where you're at if you are to develop new skills for yourself. What is missing for you? Nothing. What is wrong with you? Nothing. Why can't you feel at peace? Everything you need is within you, you just haven't recognized it.

CHAPTER 10

No Past or Future

When we stop dwelling on the past and future, two-thirds of our stress, two-thirds of our distractions, and two-thirds of our thoughts will subside by themselves.

DON'T FOLLOW THE MIND

WE TRAIN the monkey mind to rest in the present moment by practicing relative shamatha. It isn't easy to train the mind, because mind can be wild and constantly curious. It wants to try everything, it wants to learn everything, it wants to know everything. But for what? It's just curiosity. On the other hand, relative shamatha will help you to know your mind. Most people don't bother to know their mind and just keep following it blindly. Whatever their mind says, they follow. When you start to know your mind, you will begin to spot how tricky it is! You will recognize, perhaps too late, that you have given it too much power over the course of your life. You have given away all your power and become a slave to your mind. We are exhausted by it. That is definite, no doubt. We do whatever mind tells us to: "Go up, go down, get upset, get grumpy, be happy, be sad." We just follow our minds all the time.

We worry too much. We worry all the time, about things that have happened in the past and what might happen in the future. Panic and fear come up because the mind is unsettled; it is juggling all these things, up and down, up and down. We have issues in our job, our family, our relationships, our health. We are a little too disturbed by it all and our mind is not calm or settled. In shamatha meditation, as we practice focusing and concentrating the mind, we start learning to recognize our thoughts and to become relaxed about them.

We can begin slowly by reducing how much we follow our thoughts, because it's hard to stop that habit. Mind goes to the past, mind goes to the future, mind goes to the present. It goes up and down through the three times constantly. You have no peace when the mind goes to the past, you have no peace when it goes to the future. According to Dzogchen, this is how we lose the inner peace we all need. We create so much distraction by allowing our thoughts to dwell on the past and worry about the future. These thoughts are like thieves that rob us of our focus. They're like pickpockets in a big city, watching the tourists, waiting for their chance—you have to watch out for them. It's the same with the mind. The mind is a thief waiting to steal your inner peace.

You need to recognize this and start changing this experience through meditation so that the mind becomes easier, lighter, and more fun. Your thoughts will be more inspiring and your mind will feel stronger and more stable. When you go to bed, close your eyes and look at your mind. You will see millions of thoughts. It's as if you've downloaded an app that constantly creates thoughts. We need to delete that app and download a new kind of app into our system, one that stops thoughts. The app we currently have only makes us confused. But really, the fewer apps you have in your system, the better.

LET GO OF THE PAST AND FUTURE

In Dzogchen, we are not looking for temporary happiness, we want everlasting happiness. We will never achieve the happiness that remains forever by following the three times; that's not possible. We have to start with shamatha and practice breaking the habit of thought. You have thoughts about the past: "I wasn't happy, I wasn't treated well." You have thoughts about the present: "I'm not happy today." You have thoughts about the future: "What will happen to me?" You have so many thoughts.

The point of shamatha is to focus the mind, which in turn lessens our mental load. Say that thoughts from the past weigh one pound, thoughts of the future weigh one pound, and thoughts in the present weigh one pound, too. We are carrying around three pounds of thoughts in our heads all the time. When we stop dwelling on the past and future, two-thirds of our stress, two-thirds of our distractions, and two-thirds of our thoughts will subside by themselves. We might still be carrying around one pound of thoughts from the present, but that's a good start.

It's possible to maintain a healthy and happy life but only if we don't go back to the past. It's important to understand that the past may have interesting stories, there may be some tough or traumatic experiences from childhood that we keep retelling ourselves, but this only causes us more stress. We have enough stress; we don't need to make our stress worse by revisiting the past. It is too far away and too long ago. Let the extra weight of those thoughts drop away.

There are many meditation methods, yogas, therapies, and special-ists that can help alleviate our mental and physical stress. They help as much as they can, but we can also help ourselves. Our situation won't improve without support on our part. You totally have the power to change. Whether your history was bad or good, wonderful or terrible, whatever happened, it's over now. Now that the past is finished, it is time to drop it and to let it go. That will be a healing act; you will feel very free when you have more space in your mind. You will feel fresher and lighter because all that dwelling on the past occupied so much of your memory.

We also have many fears in relation to the future—the fear of death, sickness, old age, change, and failure. The mind is constantly telling us to worry. It's all part of mind's business to tell you that you must worry, you must be careful, you might get sick, you might die. The mind keeps telling you these things! We can protect ourselves from this stress by refusing to let the mind go to the future. We should stop worrying about the future because when we look toward the future, we forget to enjoy the present moment. Worry won't help you; it only makes you depressed and unstable.

Even on an everyday level, we can't enjoy our lives if the mind is always worrying about the future. You don't enjoy your breakfast because you're worrying about lunch. Your mind has already gone to the supermarket, fretting over what to cook for lunch or what food you'll need to buy. You imagine the supermarket shelves and think about what is gluten-free or sugar-free. Your body is in the present, but your mind is not. That is an unnecessary kind of stress. You can't even enjoy your breakfast. You keep on looking for the next thing without enjoying the present moment.

Enjoy the Present Moment

There is a lot we want to accomplish in our lives and we have so many thoughts about what that entails. That may be unavoidable, but we can still accomplish these tasks without stress. Stress makes the mind unfocused. When we don't focus on the moment, we are not living in the present; we are all over the place. You might have a feeling of sadness that comes from thoughts of the past or you may worry about the future. You need to cut these concerns for the past and the future and remain in the middle. Don't go to past feelings, don't go to future feelings, just feel what is in the present. That's a good start.

The future is not yet here, but the future does depend on what you do now. Farmers plant seeds and trust they will yield the expected crops within a certain timeframe. The farmer can't see this result at first, because they are starting with such small seeds. But while a seed may be small, it can still grow into a giant tree. It would be silly to assume you need a huge seed to produce a huge tree. In the same way, even a small spark can create a massive fire. We have a lot of bushfires nowadays in the world, it has become a big issue. A bushfire doesn't necessarily start big; even a burning ember can be the cause of great destruction. When something is small, that doesn't necessarily mean it doesn't have much power. Small often has more power than big. A small seed has the power to grow a giant tree and a small spark has the power to burn a whole forest. It's the same thing with our thoughts. People sometimes say,

"Oh, this is just a small thing, it's nothing to worry about," but that small thing causes us so much suffering and takes up so much of our mental space.

Just enjoy today and stop dwelling on the past or worrying about the future. We have to accept that life is very complicated and things always seem to go the opposite to what we have planned. In our world, the blind lead the blind, so don't get surprised or shocked when plans don't work out. You can't change that things are complicated, but you can learn to live within that more happily. As the great eighth-century Indian master Shantideva says in *The Way of the Bodhisattva*, you can't find enough leather to cover the entire world, but you can cover your feet in leather.

We can let go of past stress and future stress, but we can't ignore present stress. You have no choice about the circumstances around your present stress but you can choose how you respond to it, so just try your best and don't worry about what other people say or think. Do what you can in life, as best you can, and leave it at that. Enjoy whatever is in front of you now and try to be as calm as possible in each moment. You will then have a calming influence on others and bring peace into your home.

CHAPTER 11

Vipashyana

When you examine the mind, you will discover that reality
is completely different from what you supposed. You have
been relying on something that doesn't exist.

INVESTIGATING REALITY

D ZOGCHEN INCLUDES both indirect meditation, in which we investigate reality, and direct meditation, where we don't investigate
reality. We discussed direct meditation in the previous chapters. We
will now turn to indirect meditation, which is a form of analytical meditation. The right view comes about from analytical meditation, but to
get that view, we first need to calm the mind through the direct meditation of shamatha, which means that the view arises from shamatha and
vipashyana together.

We usually blindly follow the mind without examining where it
comes from. Do you know where mind comes from? Nobody knows.
Do you know where mind stays? Nobody has discovered that either. Do
you know where it goes? Nobody can say. We just keep following it anyway. That's the problem; we are following something we don't know at
all. We assume there is something there and we just keep following. We
should investigate things and recognize the real state of our mind or we
will continue to follow it without knowing what we are doing.

We investigate reality through analytical meditation to gain the extraordinary view. When you realize the true state of your mind, you will have the right view, but for the moment, you don't have that view. You are just assuming things and following your everyday experiences, thinking, "Yes, my mind is here in my head; my body is here; I can see everything around me. I feel happy and sad and all sorts of emotions." When you examine the mind, you will discover that reality is completely different from what you supposed. You have been relying on something that doesn't exist. This is the issue behind all our emotional problems and stress.

We need to break our chain of thoughts if we are to see where we are and what we believe in. We can do it by examining the evidence, as you'll see below. Things only seem real when you don't examine them, but they dissolve under investigation. We have physical evidence, common-sense evidence, logical evidence, and wisdom evidence—they all help us to see the absolute truth.

EXAMINING THE "I"

The first thing we need to understand is who we are. Where does the "I" come from? Where does it stay? Where does it go? When you examine the "I," you can't find it. When you don't examine it, the "I" pops up. You need to keep asking, "Who is this I? Where is this I? Where does it come from? Where does it stay? Where does it go?" This is not to say you are asking whether you have a name, passport, or ID; that is not the question here. You need to examine who you are in essence. This is very important.

You might say, "This 'I' can't be found when examined." But when you don't examine it, the "I" is there! Is there something wrong with this? No. Is it so important to find this "I" when you look? No. It's not a matter of being able to catch the "I." You are only being asked to examine the "I" and recognize where it comes from, where it stays, and where it goes. You will experience how illusive you are when you fail to find it because the "I" dissolves under investigation. We think, "I am here;" but when we look for this "I," we can't say anything is there at all. There is no one to recognize the "I" and no "I" to be recognized. There is no one to recognize buddha nature and no one to be buddha. All of that is just thoughts.

EXAMINING THE SENSES

The same unfindability occurs with the senses. You may hear a pleasant sound and believe it's a sound, but you need to ask, "What is a sound?" Sound is in the mind; it is baseless, rootless, and groundless. You might experience a pleasant or unpleasant smell. Again you should ask yourself, "What is a smell?" It also comes from mind. You might experience delicious, sweet, sour, or bitter tastes. Where is the temple of taste? The mind. It's the same with feelings. All five senses come from mind, and they are all baseless, rootless, and groundless. The only thing missing is that we don't recognize this for what it is.

There is nothing to see from your eyes, hear from your ears, smell from your nose, taste on your tongue, or feel on your body. But unless you analyze and examine both the "self" that experiences these and the phenomena themselves, you will always perceive something there and you will believe it. It's the same as being in a hot desert where you see a mirage—only when you get to this oasis, there is no water, there is nothing. We similarly experience things as real, but when we examine them, there is nothing to be found.

We create this very powerful influence through our senses and we believe everything that comes through them. We perceive things through our senses and develop our experiences of pleasure and pain, likes and dislikes, and become strongly affected by them. But who is telling us that something is good or not good? It's your mind. "I" decided. "I" decided this is good music. "I" decided this is a bad smell. "I" decided this is a good color. But who even is this "I," anyway? We grasp after this "I" all the time and believe in its existence. That self-grasping is ignorance. It is the root of illusion.

EXAMINING THE MIND

Everything we experience is mind, so we have to understand and recognize mind, examining it thoroughly. The first step is to ask, "Where does mind come from?" You won't find an origin. Then ask, "Where does mind stay?" You won't find anywhere for mind to stay. When you are looking for where the mind stays, you should also ask, "Does it have any physical shape? Does it have any color?" You will not find any characteristics to call mind. There is nothing like that anywhere. It has no location, no shape, and no color. The third step is to ask, "Where does mind go?" There is nowhere for it to go.

When you examine mind, you won't find it, because mind dissolves under examination. When you don't examine mind, it pops up. As soon as you get distracted, mind is there and starts to lead you straight away. It's interesting to see how clever mind is about staying with us. We are coerced by our mind and do everything it tells us. Who is telling you to go to bed? Your mind. Who is telling you to work hard? Your mind. Who is telling you to be stressed? Your mind. Who is saying you should be happy? It's your mind, nobody else. Mind comes from nowhere, it has nowhere to go and nowhere to stay, but if you don't examine it, mind is there.

It's important to continue your investigations: "Who is experiencing suffering and happiness? Who is experiencing all these things?" Do we experience these things because mind exists? Or do we experience them because it doesn't exist? That is a very interesting question. You need to cross-examine mind from all sides like this. You might conclude that all your happiness and suffering comes from mind. But then you need to ask, "Is that the mind that was born somewhere or the mind that was never born?" Can suffering come from something you can't find when you look for it?

Once you have examined mind in these ways, ask yourself, "Who is examining the mind?" This is another way of analyzing it. There are these two ways of gaining insight: examining the mind with the mind, and then examining who is doing the examination. There is nowhere for mind to go and there is no one to go. Nowhere to go, nowhere to stay, and nowhere to come from. You will finally come to recognize there is no mind to be examined and no one to examine it. You will have realized the real secret of mind when you can no longer say, "My mind exists," or "There is someone to examine mind." There is nothing like that to be found at all. Reality is beyond that.

EXAMINING EXTERNAL PHENOMENA

This unfindability is also true for external phenomena. Without your eyes, your mind could not see the phenomenal world. The eyes make the ocean, sun, moon, and stars real for you. The mind says, "My eyes can see it, so that's how it is." Except we need to stop seeing the world through our beliefs and start seeing things as they are. Our senses connect us to the world, but nobody has been able to prove yet that what our eyes see is ultimately true. The Dzogchen teachings tell us that what you see through your eyes is illusion. Nothing that you see is true, you just believe it to be true, because you perceive it. That is your evidence. The mountains, rocks, and all phenomena on the earth are called "the objects of illusion." We currently have the habit of seeing the objects of illusion as solid and so we see them as real. This habit is so strong for us. However, when you examine any object in the world, you will not be able to find it. If someone were to ask, "What is the ocean? Where does it come from?" you would not be able to answer. When you look at the ocean, it is there, but when you examine it, it dissolves.

EMPTINESS

The phenomenal world is fake reality because everything is unreal when we examine it. That doesn't mean things are not there at all, it just means they are not there when you examine them. When left unexamined, however, they are there. This is how we realize that the real state of our mind is emptiness. It's important to understand what this term *emptiness* means. Emptiness doesn't mean an object is empty *of* something.

Usually, when we say that something is empty, we are making a reference to the absence of something else. For example, we can say the table is empty, because there was a bowl on it earlier but now that's gone. In Dzogchen, emptiness means there was nothing before, there is nothing now, and there will be nothing later. There was nothing there from the very beginning.

Proponents of some Buddhist schools talk about emptiness in terms of a table being ultimately empty but still think it was there somehow in the past and it will still be there in the future. In Dzogchen, emptiness means subject and object are equally illusory. The bowl is not there, the table is not there, and you are not there. We are not saying something was there but now you need to see it as empty. Nothing was ever there, so there is nothing to be made empty.

The trees you see outside your window are not there and the one who sees the trees is not there. The trees outside your window are created by your own mind. The trees are not there, but neither is the one who is creating the trees. Mind itself is an illusion. If you say, "The trees are not there but my mind is there," you have misunderstood. The one who is seeing the trees is the mind, and the mind is the one who is creating the trees. When you examine your mind, you cannot find it, but when you don't examine it, your mind pops up. Everything that we experience is emptiness, so when we recognize, we recognize emptiness, nothing else.

There is a story of a Buddhist practitioner who meditated on emptiness for thirty years. He went to see a Dzogchen master to tell him about his retreat. The Dzogchen master thought he was a bit arrogant and was a little worried. The practitioner told him, "I did thirty years of meditation on emptiness. If you play a trumpet in my ear, I will not hear it. If ten thousand cows run in front of my eyes, I will not see them." The Dzogchen master thought, "My goodness, he has just wasted thirty years." He told the practitioner, "If you have ears but can't hear sound, you are deaf. If you have eyes but can't see animals, you are blind. You don't need a thirty-year retreat to achieve that. Anyone can do it!"

Emptiness doesn't mean there is nothing there at all. We are not grasping after nothingness. We aren't saying something is there or that something is not there. We cannot say "it is there" because even buddhas do not see it, and we cannot say "it is not there" because it appears. It is just that everything is our perception. Both samsara and nirvana are created by this perception. Reality is beyond language and beyond judgment. This subject of emptiness usually leads to a very philosophical level of debate among various Buddhist schools, but in Dzogchen, such discourse is futile because there is nothing to debate.

ILLUSION

When you examine things, you are using your wisdom, and you find that things dissolve by themselves. But when you don't examine things, you are not using your wisdom, and your ignorance creates all these appearances, beliefs, and negative emotions. We need to break that ignorance and recognize that everything in the mental and material worlds is illusion. We create so many things, it's important to examine that tendency and gain some real experience of it; doing so will be a seed for the continued growth of your own strength and wisdom.

We can prove the illusoriness of things in different ways. We can prove it with the intellect and we can prove it beyond the intellect. We need evidence to disprove what we have believed in for so long, to see that those beliefs are just our habits. Sometimes we prove our beliefs to be wrong, but we still want to believe them because it's more comfortable to keep doing the same old thing. In Tibet we have the saying, "Pigs believe they live in the pure realms when their pigsty is really a filthy mess." We also think we live in the right place but we do not.

Logic can support us to see that phenomena are unreal, but it can only take us so far. We also need to believe phenomena are unreal, which is very difficult for us. Analytical meditation will help us believe in that unreality, it will help break the habit of believing in illusion. Reality itself is beyond language and beyond mind, so we can't judge it with the mind at all.

Things affect us because we are not good enough at resting within the state of illusion. We start to dissolve our belief in the reality of this illusion through vipashyana meditation. We find that mind doesn't come from anywhere and there is no one to look for it. We have problems when we believe things are real, so it's important to experience the unreality of things. We can only do that through meditation. When you examine who and where you are, the "I" dissolves, but if you don't examine it, the "I" pops up. Every object is the same; every flower, tree, mountain, and river will dissolve under examination, but if you don't examine it, it will pop up. There is no subject and no object, they are complete emptiness, yet they appear. This is the magical display of the mind.

As soon as you recognize that the "I" and external appearances do not exist, you will experience incredible clarity, peace, and power. You will feel connected to all sentient beings spontaneously because we are all interconnected on a deeper level. This experience cannot be compared to anything else because it's beyond the measurement of our relative structures. When you realize the illusory nature of all phenomena, your mind will no longer be confined within samsara. You will merge into the heart of the buddhas and be able to help all sentient beings spontaneously. There will be nobody there to feel lonely or sad. The whole story will be complete, finished; the drama is gone, you have gone beyond it. You have the extraordinary view.

CHAPTER 12

Let Come, Let Go

When something is difficult or not working out for you,
just accept it and it will get easier. Let come, let go.
Don't follow your thoughts, your stories, your narratives.

TURN YOUR MIND INWARD

WE USE the mind to analyze the mind, but can we find it? No way. Buddhist teachings say not even the buddhas could find the mind, so how are we going to find it? It's impossible, but we try to pinpoint it anyway because we always want to know more. Our intellectual mind likes to know everything. While it is important to practice analytical meditation, we need to go beyond the intellect and rest the analyzing mind. When the analyzing mind is completely at rest, there is nothing to analyze, and no one to analyze it. We discussed relative shamatha and the value of using our concentration to remain in the present moment. This is important, but this is only stage one in Dzogchen practice. The next stage of Dzogchen shamatha is to recognize each thought as it arises.

We gain wisdom by letting the mind remain calm. If we think that something is a problem, we will get stressed by it, and then wisdom will not arise. We need to give our thoughts space. Sometimes mind is happy, sometimes it's sad. It can be happy in the morning and grumpy in the afternoon. This is not to judge right and wrong here, we just need to recognize the way it is. That is the nature of human beings, so you don't need to worry about it. You are allowed to be grumpy, just as you are allowed to be kind, too. Sometimes you feel kind and you want to be kind. Sometimes you feel grumpy. That's our nature, and it's good to recognize the fact that you have both aspects.

We are learning to watch our minds and notice whatever thought comes up without reacting to it. Notice it, but don't make a big deal of it, or you will start thinking, "I must do something—I must challenge this." How many years have you been doing that? It's never going to end unless you turn your mind inward and watch it every day. Stop looking at everyone else and look at yourself. Watch your own mind and see how many thoughts come up. The mind has so many thoughts, it's like a bustling international airport with thousands of people coming and going all the time.

We need to identify the types of emotions that arise because many different emotions come and go every day. Look at how we deal with emotions such as anger and jealousy. Anger is never good for you; it's a powerful negative emotion and a powerful energy. Anger is not bad in itself, but it gives rise to aggression, jealousy, and pride, which is why it is called one of the five poisons. Anger is considered a poison because of what results come from it; we turn it into poison. It can destroy us and it can destroy our friendships and relationships.

Anger is easy to recognize, but jealousy is a different problem and quite dangerous. We call it the "silent" emotion because it's hidden behind a facade, a bit like a snake. You never know when a snake is coming for you; you need to keep vigilant around a snake or it might suddenly rear up and bite you. Jealousy can rise up like that and destroy your relationships, your friendships, and your sense of peace. When we examine it, we can see that jealousy is all about ourselves. We are always thinking, "I want to be happy. They are happy, why not me?"

What do you do when an emotion arises? To begin with, just recognize the emotion. Don't judge it, just recognize it for what it is. Just as you identify different types of drinks, like soda, juice, or water, in order to choose the most suitable one, we recognize our thoughts and emotions in order to be able to discriminate between them. Recognition allows you to make the right choice. We need to recognize our thoughts and emotions so that we know when anger, pride, attachment, desire, or jealousy are present.

DON'T BLOCK, DON'T FOLLOW

All those negative emotions and thoughts are just the drama of the mind. It never ends. We need to get rid of these thoughts and feelings, but we can't force them to go, we can't push them away, that's not possible. Most schools of Buddhism will say that when negative emotions come, we should block them, and when positive emotions come, we should follow them. It's easy to say, "Block your negative thoughts," but they only get worse when you do. Dzogchen never advises us to block our thoughts and emotions or to deny their existence.

The special method of Dzogchen is to let our thoughts and emotions come without following them, because following them only creates a storyline that gets bigger and feels more solid. The Dzogchen teachings say that whatever arises—good thoughts or bad thoughts, good emotions or bad emotions—let it come, but don't follow it. In Dzogchen, good thoughts are still just thoughts, so we don't judge them as being better than negative thoughts. The Dzogchen approach is to say, "No matter what thought or emotion arises, don't do anything. Just let it come and let it go." If you can do that, you will not be stressed by thoughts. We call that the practice of "let come, let go." We don't want any thoughts. No thought in the mind, no cloud in the sky. It's a lot of fun.

Every hour we have so many thoughts. That's important to acknowledge. Don't be panicked by all these thoughts, just let come, let go. All the negative emotions will come, and that's okay. Don't block them and don't follow them. You may notice you have a lot of fear. But we can't block fear from the mind—it will just come back bigger and stronger. Just let come, let go. Don't block fear and don't follow fear. Don't invite good thoughts and don't reject bad thoughts. Stop worrying about all the things that come up in your mind. Recognize your thoughts, let them come, and let them go. If you follow your negative emotions, they will drive you mad, so it's better not to follow them. If you block your negative emotions, they will only get worse, so don't block them. Don't do anything with them at all. Just let them come, let them go. Then they won't be a big deal.

THREE STAGES OF RECOGNIZING THOUGHTS

Normally, if we are unable to block our negative thoughts, we follow them. We know it's no good to follow them, that it's no good to follow anger, jealousy, pride, or ego—ego is the worst thing to follow, it's a poison—but we do it anyway, out of habit. We think, "I can't change, this is how I always do things." Our habits have nothing to do with who we are, they are just what we are used to doing. How are you going to adapt your view? How are you going to break your old "pick and choose" habit and change it to a "let come, let go" habit?

When something is difficult or not working out for you, just accept it and it will get easier. Let come, let go. Don't follow your thoughts, your stories, your narratives. Whether thoughts are happy or sad, good or bad, they all have the same compelling repetition. Just watch them.

We often think that we're not good enough or not strong enough, but we need to break that habit. You *are* good enough. You *are* strong enough. You have everything you need. This is not just positive thinking. It's the truth. We need to break the habit of believing in the relative, intellectual mind. Our tendency to like this and not that is what keeps us trapped in our habits. If we develop right view by learning to let come, let go, that view will break the power habits have over us. We are normally led by habits and it seems very difficult to change them. Now is the time to change them, the time to end them. We practice Dzogchen shamatha so we can learn to let go. We've had enough of stress and distractions.

There are three stages to our meditation practice. Firstly, we need to recognize each thought as it arises in the mind and learn to recognize its familiarity. Then, we start to see that those thoughts simply resolve by themselves if we leave them alone. Finally, we come to understand that our thoughts are harmless because there is no one to be affected by them.

Stage 1:
Thoughts are like old friends

We need to immediately recognize our habitual thought patterns, the ones that return again and again, as old friends. We want to come to a place where we can say, "I know this anger," "I know this trickiness," "I know this jealousy," "I know this joy." When these thoughts arise it is like meeting an old friend, someone you know very well. We all have anger, jealousy, desire, and pride. When you identify jealousy arising, say to yourself, "My mind is quite tricky, but I recognize this jealousy as my old friend. I will stay away from this situation until it's gone." Jealousy is quite complicated, but you must let it go, seeing it as useless. Instead, just be yourself—enjoy life and have fun. What is jealousy anyway? Things don't just belong to you, they belong to all of us. We are a unity, we are one. It's no good being so separate and individualistic to the point where you feel jealousy over what someone else has. If you can be more open, you will enjoy yourself more and more.

We become more open by noticing our habitual thoughts and recognizing them as our old friends. If you can recognize a thought as an old friend, you will see that you already know it and you will be able to handle it. Now, it's okay to explain that thought or emotion to yourself, but try not to express it outwardly. For example, when anger arises, just think, "There you are my old friend." Anger is a very tricky friend. You can't trust it. It's like a guest that will trash your house.

Stage 2:
Thoughts will fix themselves

At the moment you recognize a thought, it is finished, it is liberated. We always think we need to do something about our problems, worries, plans, and anxieties, but if you just leave the thoughts alone—if you let come, let go—your problems will resolve by themselves. If you tie a snake into a knot, you don't need to go back and untie it; the snake will unknot by itself. If you recognize a thought and leave it alone, it will also unravel by itself. You don't need to fix it. You don't need to do anything.

Stage 3:
Thoughts are like thieves in an empty house

When you recognize your thoughts as old friends and let them unravel by themselves, you no longer have anything to lose. Nor do you have anything to gain, so every thought that arises is incapable of harming you. If a thief breaks into your house when it's empty, you have nothing to worry about because there will be nothing to steal. You can relax. Whether a thief comes or not, it's no big deal, it doesn't bother you. Thoughts come and thoughts go. When you no longer block or follow your thoughts, they will no longer bother you, you will have nothing to lose and nothing to fear. You will be completely beyond that.

You worry now because you have so many possessions in your house. You not only need to make sure your house is locked but that your garden is watered, and your gas, electricity, and insurance bills have been paid. It's such a headache and the more you have, the more your head aches. When you are young parents, you need a big house for your kids, and then when the kids grow up and leave, you still need to maintain the house. You have become a slave to the house. We become stuck in a pattern and just repeat the same things over and over.

An empty mind is like that empty house you don't need to lock. If you have an empty mind, you don't need to guard it. You have nothing to lose—no illusion of identity, no illusion of goals, illusion of wealth, illusion of property, illusion of possessions. So when anger arises, you need to notice it and let come, let go. That is like recognizing a thief in your house. If you see the thief, they won't steal anything and if you recognize the anger, it won't be able to steal your better judgment. Everything will be a blessing—your happiness, your suffering, your obstacles—because the house is empty.

TRUST THE PROCESS

You may find that you are at the stage of being able to recognize your thoughts as old friends, but you are not yet able to allow your thoughts to fix themselves. You think you need to fix them because your ego is still there. Ego tells us, "I have to fix it, because I'm here." You don't need to fix them; they will get fixed by themselves. You could also have trust in the buddhas and let them fix it. The buddhas are there for a reason. Let the buddhas fix it for you. Buddha is the absolute truth anyway. If you have a lot of stress from health or family issues or something else, please don't stress. If stress does come, just let it come, but don't follow it. Let Buddha look after your stress, you don't need to deal with it. Of course, once you have fully realized your inner buddha, you can take the stress—it won't affect you. If you haven't yet recognized you are buddha, stress can really harm you, so do not stress. Your thoughts, emotions, and problems will sort themselves out, you don't need to do anything.

You don't need to worry about your life or about what will happen; worry does not help you. Just see whatever happens as a blessing. Suffering is a blessing, happiness is a blessing, obstacles are a blessing. Whatever comes is a blessing when you know that you are free. There is nothing to worry about—it is just a matter of making a clear decision about what you want to do. The house is empty. Well, your house may not be empty yet, but it could be quite soon. You need to recognize that you own this incredible wisdom, this incredible power. Just like an eagle flying high up in the sky, you will have an entire view of the landscape instead of a limited one.

CHAPTER 13

The Incredible Gap

Mind becomes naked mind. There are no thoughts
of the future, no thoughts of the past, no
thoughts of the present.

FINDING THE PAUSE BUTTON

THE PAST, present, and future are created by mind and we need to
break the habit of believing in them. Mind thinks that time exists
because everybody believes it is there, but this habit of time will never
let us be free. It is in the practice of meditation that we break that habit.
If mind doesn't go to the past, present, and future, then the three times
have no reality. The future is not there, the past is not there, and the
present is not there either. If you pause time, you will not even move
in the now. When we finally see that we alone create the three times
and are just following something that is our own creation, we come to
understand that we give ourselves no time to rest. We are busy and tired
and complain that we "don't have time," but time does not exist. We
made time up!

A DVD player has several functions, including play, fast-forward,
rewind, and pause. Likewise, we have these functions—and we can stay
in the present moment and enjoy having pressed "play" without rewind-
ing or pressing the fast-forward button. Staying in the present is more
fun than going to the past or future anyway. Otherwise, you will have so
much stress from the past. You think about what has happened in your

life: "Oh, just look at what happened, I want revenge, I want to have a debate with someone." You get caught up in remembering how somebody did something wrong to you, and now you want to prove it, you want to challenge them. And you will also have stress if you keep letting the mind go to the future, thinking about your plans and how to achieve them. It's like you are taking a shower in your thoughts.

Relative shamatha practice promotes the play button, but now we are promoting the pause button. This is the next stage of Dzogchen. Pause is the best button; it is the most excellent function. When you press pause you have no drama. Along with cutting thoughts about the past and thoughts of the future, the pause button also cuts present thoughts. The rewind, fast-forward, and play buttons will all be immobilized. That pause gives you a real experience; you discover a time where nothing changes, where all is calm, peaceful, and still. That pause is the fourth time, the timeless time. All thoughts dissolve when we rest in that timelessness. We will have more space and more freedom because we know that time is an illusion.

When you rest the mind in that pause, it won't give rise to thoughts, because thoughts are based in the three times. You recognize the unity of absolute time by letting go of past, present, and future while resting the mind. When you rest the mind, time also rests. When time rests, it's amazing! You feel very still, calm, and powerful. You have cut the chain of thoughts completely and are free, like a clear and cloudless sky.

Pausing is the real practice because this is where we have real experience. We usually live on karmic ground, in karmic time, because karma is what creates time. We create karma, karma creates time, and then we experience suffering and happiness, as well as old age, sickness, and death. Time allows you to experience these things. If time were unchanging, none of these things would happen, you would just remain at peace. There would be nothing else to experience. Dzogchen is like a pause; with this practice you remain completely still, and there is no changing, no moving. Time is a stable presence.

Resting in the Gap

Take a moment to experience this for yourself. Relax your body and settle into the meditation posture. You can sit on the ground with legs crossed, or simply sit in a comfortable chair and rest your hands on your knees. You can lean back slightly and breathe from the mouth, not the nostrils. Rest your gaze straight ahead or slightly upward at the blue sky. The key method is to breathe in naturally from the mouth, then breathe out and hold the out-breath for a few seconds. You breathe in again before it becomes uncomfortable, then breathe out and hold the out-breath for a few seconds. Holding the out-breath for those seconds is called the "moment of pause," because during that moment it is impossible to give rise to thoughts.

We call that state of pause a gap. We breathe out through the mouth, hold the breath, and find the perfect gap. This gap in our thoughts is important because our mind is always leading us, always influencing us and demanding things. When you hold the breath, the mind is very still. It is naked mind. There are no thoughts; there is no past, present, or future. We need to let go of this mind a bit and tell it to calm down. All our problems come from the mind. The mind makes life difficult, it makes enemies, it makes problems for others, it makes a mess in the world. When you calm your mind, you can create that incredible gap, and this allows common sense to guide you. You can help others and contribute good energy into the world.

We need mental space to create this gap, which is why we start by learning relative shamatha. As we learn to let come, let go, we start to create the space that disrupts our never-ending chain of thoughts. When we have millions of thoughts, one after another, we will never have the space to create a gap. The gap is what gives you an experience of clarity. This meditation is absolute shamatha. You gain that clarity by resting the mind in the gap. This is the real Dzogchen meditation.

When you breathe in, you have air in your lungs. We call that "life." When you breathe out, you have no air in your lungs. We call that "death." Both of those moments are interesting in meditation because you experience life and death together. When you hold your out-breath, that's what we call the gap. Dzogchen meditation is about looking for that gap. That gap is beyond the mind. It is absolute reality. It is the same as rigpa, our nondual pure awareness. Our rigpa is always present, but we need to catch it in the gap, almost like putting a golf ball into a hole. You breathe in, breathe out, hold the out-breath, and putt your mind into the gap. That moment of holding the breath is the gap. The gap is a pause with no thoughts, no movement; it is completely and permanently still.

MAINTAINING THE GAP

The real practice to cultivate is maintaining this awareness and staying in it for as long as you can. If you can maintain that awareness, that's it! You don't need to do anything. Breathe in, breathe out, and hold the out-breath for a moment, a few seconds maybe, or as long as you feel comfortable. There is no movement of energy in that moment because your karmic energy has stopped. Karmic energy rides on the breath and it's no longer moving when you hold the breath. Everything is still, mind is completely empty of thought. You don't even need to think about the gap experience. Everything you need is there. That's the moment when you see the face of a buddha.

Dzogchen meditation is really about how long you can stay in this gap. We progress slowly with this practice. It is risky to stay for too long, because breathing is part of life. It's important for you to experience this gap, to get a momentary glimpse of it, so you can come to identify it: "Here you are." You will know there is no name or description for this experience. It's beyond language, beyond words, it's incredible.

If you sometimes have a lot of thoughts and stress, you can breathe out sharply and say, "PHET!" on the out-breath, quite forcefully. It's as if your thoughts were water running through a hose and the syllable PHET was a sharp sword that cut straight through it so the stream of thoughts is stopped. Whenever you breathe in and hold the out-breath, you will experience a moment of peace. The PHET! tries to catch that moment of peace so that you have a clear view in the gap.

Take a moment to see what you experience when you hold the breath. This is not about what you feel but what you experience. Is it something completely calm and peaceful, something without movement? Mind becomes naked mind. There are no thoughts of the future, no thoughts of the past, no thoughts of the present. This is a very important gap. This is meditation, nothing else. The more you are able to maintain this gap, the better your meditation will be. In this moment of the gap you'll experience everlasting happiness rather than mundane happiness. In that moment of the gap, even time is still; there is no change, no movement. Breathing in and out is illusion; the gap is not an illusion. The gap is the main foundation of Dzogchen.

It can be hard to maintain the gap for long because our minds are distracted so easily and we need to breathe in again. Whenever we breathe in, we are born again. When we breathe out, we die. We sometimes fear holding our out-breath in the gap for fear we are going to die. We rely on breathing because breathing is energy and movement. That is samsara. There is no movement in enlightenment.

When you move out of the gap, you become part of the present again, and your mind goes to the future, to the past, and to the present. The gap will be gone. Maybe you can't stay in the gap for too long yet, but you can stay there sometimes; you will gradually learn to stay there much longer until you can comfortably rest in that state. The more you can maintain that state, the better. Calm your mind, then maintain that calm for as long as you can without thought.

WISDOM

This gap may seem like a small seed of something greater, but it is very powerful. In that moment, you no longer believe your dualistic perceptions and gain a fleeting glimpse of an incredible peace that is beyond language. Clarity gives you that experience. From time to time, you will have spontaneous experiences of spaciousness and peace, but these spontaneous experiences only happen when you are resting in the gap, and there is no reason or purpose to them. That is Dzogchen practice. That is the experience of buddha nature. When your thoughts dissolve in that moment, wisdom can arise.

We have wisdom already, but we need the space to recognize it. The mind and wisdom always go together. We can take the example of smoke and fire to understand how this works. You know there is a fire when you can say, "I see smoke over there." If there is smoke, there must be fire. In the same way, if there is a mind, there must be wisdom. There is no mind without wisdom. That's very necessary to understand. Smoke comes from fire; fire never comes from smoke. Similarly, the mind comes from wisdom. That's how it is.

You have wisdom within you, but it can't lead if you don't concentrate the mind. Only ignorance will lead you. You need to minimize the thoughts and stress in your mind so that it becomes very clear, like a cloudless sky. When the mind is free of thoughts, it has a lot of space and peace. That is how wisdom and concentration go together. Wisdom is there, but if you don't concentrate, wisdom will not be able to lead you. Your meditation is perfect when wisdom can lead. When mind is leading you, you are a sentient being. When mind is resting, you are a buddha. You experience that moment of resting in the gap. That moment is enlightenment.

CHAPTER 14

Resting the Mind

We can write words in the sky without being
able to read them and we can call something
"meditation" without being able to see it.

ONE MIND

WE CONCENTRATE on the method of breathing in and out because it creates the space for the mind to rest. The relative shamatha techniques of mindfulness and concentration are important, but the best meditation is the breathing technique to rest the mind. Nobody has found a better meditation yet. As Patrul Rinpoche, the nineteenth-century Tibetan master, said, "The past buddhas never found a better method, so how could I find one?" Remaining calm and resting the mind is one of the key points of Dzogchen. It's the main thing, really, and it helps us so much. It is easier to just go directly to the mind as a way of recognizing emptiness. In analytical meditation we think, "I am a person, but this person isn't real, so I am emptiness." But that is a tough way go about believing in emptiness. If you go directly to the mind, it doesn't matter if you are somebody or nobody, you rest the mind and see the illusoriness of the person.

When your mind is calm and resting, everything becomes like a reflection of the moon in a lake. All phenomena are reflections in the mind, and when mind is resting, we can see that they are not real. The moon represents nondual awareness and its reflection in the lake represents dual awareness. It's all illusion, but as it is reflected in our minds, we can't ignore it. We believe in many minds because of this, but there is only one mind. All of your experiences are just mind, and when you understand this, you transcend subject and object.

ENLIGHTENMENT WITHOUT MEDITATION

Dzogchen meditation is very interesting; it looks like you almost don't need to make any effort at all. As Guru Rinpoche, the eighth-century Indian tantric master renowned in Tibet as the second Buddha, says, "There is nothing to meditate on." All the buddhas introduced enlightenment through meditation, but Guru Rinpoche introduced an effortless vehicle that we call "enlightenment without meditation." Meditation techniques typically require hard work. That is not the case in Dzogchen. We just rest the mind. It's that simple.

We call resting the mind a "meditation," but that is just a label. There is nothing to meditate on, so there is really nothing to do. You just rest the mind in the gap without thoughts. You don't have anything to focus on, you don't have any technique to follow, you don't have anything specific to realize. We can write words in the sky without being able to read them and we can call something "meditation" without being able to see it. We can have a label even if we can't pinpoint what we are labeling. It's just incredible. There is something, there is nothing; but nothingness is a somethingness.

Don't misunderstand this effortlessness and think that Dzogchen is just about being lazy. "Doing nothing" has been misunderstood in the past and can be misunderstood in the present. We have so many thoughts and we usually just follow them wherever they lead us. When I say "do nothing," I mean don't do anything with your thoughts. Don't block them, don't follow them, don't hold on to them. You can still do things to help with Dzogchen meditation—you can focus the mind and calm the mind—but you are "doing nothing" when you stop following thoughts. You can cook, you can drive, you can walk; everything can be done with a calm mind that is resting. The view you have when you are resting the mind will give you inspiration and help you have more fun and less stress. We can learn so many great things from resting.

PURE FROM THE BEGINNING

Various Buddhist traditions have many stages of understanding that all tell us we aren't perfect, and we need to become perfect. Only Dzogchen says that we don't need to do anything except go back to where we came from, to our true condition. You just need to recognize how it was. That's it. You don't need to change anything, you don't need to do anything, all you need is recognition. This "recognition" means to see who you are, to see that you are already perfect and you don't need to *become* perfect. The Dzogchen term for this is *kadag*, which in Tibetan means "pure from the beginning." It doesn't make sense to say that something that isn't pure will become pure. That might make sense from a relative perspective, but not from an absolute one. The Dzogchen teachings say that to think something is not pure now but will become pure later is just being intellectual.

If something is not pure, it is not pure. Our true nature is kadag, pure from the beginning. It never changes. It is permanently pure. We just need to recognize this purity; we don't need to change, we are already perfect. We just need to go back to where we came from. That is our challenge. That's why we always have Samantabhadra, the blue one, depicted in the center of Dzogchen thangkas. Samantabhadra represents being pure from the beginning. Samantabhadra is painted blue, the color of the sky, to represent that beginningless perfection.

Dzogchen is a very interesting way to reach enlightenment. It's a direct approach where you experience the path in a different way. The Dzogchen teachings never claim, "You will get enlightenment sometime in the future." They say, "You will get it now, you will experience it now, you will get the taste now." You just start resting the mind now, and once you start, you continue. That's the difference. Dzogchen is very precise, it is direct and simple. That's why it is so incredible.

Even though we are perfect from the beginning, sometimes we are confused and lost. Luckily, you have realized that you are lost. That is a good start. Most sentient beings in this world don't understand that. You must look at where you came from and go back to the root. You aren't looking for a new place, you are looking for the original place, which is the place you have lost. In Dzogchen, we call this the "meeting of mother and child." The child became lost from the mother, but that recognition is the child returning, so they are safely together again. That's how we describe going back to where we originate.

The Nature of Mind

We need to separate mind from the nature of mind, because mind and the nature of mind are different systems. Mind is the intellectual mind, the complicated samsaric mind, but when that mind is at rest, it goes beyond relative experiences and reveals the nature of mind. Mind is very powerful—it can process things, it can move our hands and feet, it controls everything. Whatever mind is doing, the nature of mind is right there with it. In Dzogchen meditation we are learning to rest the samsaric mind so that we can reach the incredible, genuine nature of mind.

There is no fear when you are within the nature of mind. When you are beyond this mind, all fear is gone. There is no fear of death because death isn't experienced there. The great masters, such as the Fourth Dzogchen Rinpoche, Mingyur Namkhai Dorje, and Dzogchen Patrul Rinpoche, had no fear, not because buddhas are special but because the nature of mind has no fear. Mind tells us to worry and fear because that is mind's business. We need to go beyond this strongly influential mind to the nature of mind.

We always want to know if we've recognized our true nature, but when you "know" you are recognizing it, you are distracted. When you are genuinely resting, you don't need to know. Why do you want to know, anyway? That is just giving power to mind. The tricky mind always says, "Trust me, don't trust your heart. I need to know." Mind can't recognize its true nature unless it's at rest, and then there is no one to recognize. You experience nonduality, where subject and object are no longer separate. There is nothing to change, nothing to improve, nowhere to go, and no one to go there.

When you recognize the true nature of mind you will discontinue the chain of thoughts that is making sure samsara never ends. You need to start by examining the relative nature of your mind, but when you examine it, you will not find it. When it comes to the absolute nature of mind, just let go of all your thoughts and you will experience it. A clear mind has no thoughts. That is perfect. Once you recognize the nature of mind, you need to maintain that recognition by remaining at rest as much as possible within that state. Can you stay there? It's possible, but distractions do come quite fast. You will get distracted, then you will go back to resting, then you will get distracted again and go back to resting, and so on.

The Difference between Resting and Relaxing

Dzogchen is not about being able to relax the mind; it is about being able to rest the mind. Relaxing the mind and resting the mind are quite different, so be careful, because people often mix them up. Relaxing has a feeling component; it's associated with the mind, because when you relax, you feel satisfied. You think, "Oh, now I'm relaxed, it feels so good." Resting doesn't include feeling, it's a different experience. It's more about peace than about how it feels. If feeling is there, you can know you are relaxing, not resting. There is a very fine line between resting in Dzogchen and resting in *alaya*, between resting and relaxing, between the wisdom of mind and the wisdom of wisdom. You need to be very careful to put these things in good order or you can mix them up and get really confused. If they are in a good order, you will gain a better view, and you will really know what you are experiencing. You will be able to feel that immediately.

Alaya is the ground of your experiences, whatever you see through your eyes that gets reflected in your mind. That reflection is the relative world, where you see things in relation to your own karmic structure—

the pre-plan of the mind that determines how you construct your world. But that isn't necessarily the truth. When you say "I saw" or "I know," it's a lie, because as soon as you say "I," it is wrong. Dzogchen meditation is about cutting through illusion and recognizing your own great potential, your own great awareness. You might go to the top of the highest mountain where you can see everything, but that is not Dzogchen. That is alaya. When you look out at the world and don't recognize it as fake, you are resting in alaya. You might think you are doing Dzogchen meditation when you look at the stars, the sun, or space, but that is only relative reality, it's not Dzogchen. In Dzogchen meditation we know that what we are looking at is an illusion. It's all just mind. It has no reality.

In Dzogchen, our main issues are all part of the illusion of relative truth, so we need to understand how the relative exists. Then we need to recognize how the absolute exists. It's quite simple: when the mind is distracted, it's "relative," and when the mind rests, it's "absolute." The more you are able to rest your mind, the more you are in the absolute; the more distracted you are, the more you are in the relative. We are very familiar with the relative nature of mind, so we follow the mind and its millions of thoughts; we grasp after past, present, and future. The absolute mind is without thoughts and does not go toward the three times. Resting the mind in the gap is how we overcome fake reality and the illusory subjects of this samsaric bubble. Illusion is broken by this little gap. Resting the mind will eradicate your belief in birth, death, rebirth, and suffering. All those things will cease to exist in that moment.

Two Puzzles

Relative shamatha and Dzogchen shamatha are quite different, even though they are both called shamatha. We started by discussing relative shamatha, where we learn to focus the mind to reduce stress, improve concentration, and stay in the present moment. We looked at mindfulness and concentration and then at analysis, where we examine where mind comes from, where it stays, and where it goes. These are all good basic trainings for the mind to become calm and to recognize illusion. Then we discussed the absolute shamatha of Dzogchen, which is about letting go of thoughts and entering the enlightenment experience. You can't just reach enlightenment in one big jump, you must go through the stages in a gradual process.

Sometimes people meditate for a long time in the completely wrong way, which is why we are very careful about what meditation we choose in Dzogchen. Dzogchen has very clear instructions for meditation, there is always a logic behind it, always a skill, always a method. Dzogchen is such a strong and powerful method, which is why it is so successful. The purpose of resting is to discover your absolute true nature, your inner buddha. You will merge with that buddha as who you are.

I have discussed these meditations, these skills, to give you a sampling. You might not need to use all of them. They are like little pieces of a jigsaw puzzle. But imagine having two jigsaw puzzles: a relative puzzle and an absolute puzzle. The pieces of the puzzles are all in a box, and the problem is they are all mixed up and you need to separate them into two pictures. The view is in the box, but it's not in good order. Once the pieces are ordered properly, you will see the relative and absolute views. Enlightenment is there, but it's all mixed up. You must put it in good order and then your enlightenment will be clear. It's already within you. We need to be independent and strong to put this puzzle together, but we always need to have a lineage and a teacher to introduce the way, nonetheless.

I hope you have gotten some of the flavor of Dzogchen from these methods. It's so practical, so incredible, so simple. Rest the body, rest the energy, and then spontaneously rest the mind. You don't need to think about it. Enlightenment is within you. Do you understand? You have it. Your buddha is inside, your true nature is inside. All you need is recognition. When you remain in the gap, without going to the past, present, or future, you will have that peaceful moment of clarity. Dark experiences of fear, worry, and doubt cannot exist in that clarity. When your mind can really rest, you will find this incredible wisdom, this wonderful clarity, within yourself. That is a kind of miracle.

CHAPTER 15

Blessings of the Lineage

You have incredible devotion. Do you recognize that?
You don't. That is the problem. It's not the quality of
your devotion that's the problem, it's the failure
to recognize devotion within yourself.

THE DZOGCHEN LINEAGE

THE DZOGCHEN TEACHINGS have deep roots. I practice the Khandro Nyingthig lineage of Dzogchen, which was brought to Tibet by Guru Rinpoche and revealed by Longchenpa as terma. This cycle of teachings has been taught in Dzogchen Monastery in Tibet for hundreds of years. Dzogchen comes from the adi-buddha Samantabhadra and has continued in an unbroken lineage to the present day. We are not guessing at the truth in these teachings, and we are not cutting and pasting teachings from one text to another. The lineage masters are handing down the key to realization. We must have trust and devotion in this incredible Dzogchen lineage. It is powerful and you will receive its blessings if you have trust. The lineage is always a solution; it's never a problem. The Dzogchen lineage doesn't want to support you artificially or intellectually. The world around you might be upside down, but the lineage is never upside down—it is always with you and supporting you. You can reach enlightenment through this lineage. Science, technology, and personal brilliance will not take you there. In fact, the more you follow your own mind, the more trouble you will have reaching it. The less you follow your mind, the quicker your progress will be.

We need to follow the lineage without questioning or doubt. We can achieve realization through the lineage with the support of a lineage master. The master is able to tell you that your pure awareness is already with you. The guru points that out to you. The guru introduces you. At the moment you don't know where your true nature is. You have to trust the method, trust the guru, and trust the lineage. If you don't trust the lineage, the introduction will not work. The student connects to the guru and the guru connects to the lineage. He or she is like the Wi-Fi that connects you to the network. This is the blessing from the lineage, the blessing from the buddhas, the blessing from Guru Rinpoche. We follow the Buddha and Guru Rinpoche. If you pray to Guru Rinpoche, he will always be with you, he will never leave you.

Devotion

Devotion is the key that opens a new door; it is an exit into a new dimension. Devotion is the switch, the entry permit, what admits you to the 3D world of the absolute view. You already have within you incredible devotion, impossible to make any bigger, but you keep this devotion shut away in the cupboard and create an artificial intellectual kind of devotion, which is very hard to maintain. It's here today and gone tomorrow. You have anger or doubts, and suddenly your devotion is lost. That isn't real devotion; it just has the label "devotion." Real devotion is inside you already. You just need to bring it out, that's all. You don't need to go somewhere to get it, you don't need to build it, you don't need to make it better. It's already perfect.

People sometimes think they are meant to be devoted to their guru as a person, but that's wrong. You need to see your guru as the form of a rainbow rather than as a physical person. The guru is the lineage. You can be inspired by someone, that's devotion too, don't get me wrong; but real devotion is absolute reality. When you are devoted to your guru, it is not in the dualistic sense of "self and other." You are trusting your own enlightenment.

Guru Rinpoche can help you recognize your devotion, but he is not helping you as who you are, he is helping you as it is. All sentient beings have the blessing of the buddhas and the blessings of Guru Rinpoche. This blessing never stops; it is always online. You don't receive it because you don't have the link, which is devotion. That is the problem. Intelligence can help you develop devotion, but only as a temporary support. Research, analysis, and meditation can all help, but when you recognize absolute devotion, intelligence is not a requirement. The intellect cannot recognize. If the intellect is present, devotion will not be there; it will dissolve.

I hear students say they don't have devotion or that their devotion needs to be better. So many have this worry. That is completely wrong— you don't need to make your devotion better. You have incredible devotion. Do you recognize that? You don't. That is the problem. It's not the quality of your devotion that's the problem, it's the failure to recognize devotion within yourself. It is already good enough. It is excellent, perfect. The only issue is you don't recognize it. We are not trying to *experience* devotion; we need to recognize it. Recognizing devotion is one of our most important challenges in Dzogchen.

INTRODUCTION

Recognition and understanding are completely different. You can't get recognition from reading a book. You can only get it from being introduced to your true nature by a qualified guru. You have been lost in illusion for so long, you need external assistance to recognize your true nature, your buddha nature, your nondual pure awareness or *rigpa*. Recognition is the method. The external assistance is the introduction.

Introduction is a powerful way to directly reveal your pure awareness, so the guru is crucial for you. We need two things to realize Dzogchen: the ground of our nondual pure awareness, which we already have, and the introduction from the guru. You can't guess at your true nature; you can't assume you know what it is. You might think, "I already have buddha nature, so why do I need a guru to tell me that?" You have been lost for so long that you need to be reintroduced to your pure awareness by someone who knows it.

The mind cannot recognize rigpa. Mind is always present, and pure awareness is always present, too, except it hardly gets used. Pure awareness is your reality, it is the genuine you, but you ignore it and prioritize an artificial intellectual awareness. You need to trust and believe the lineage instead of trusting the tricky mind. The lineage will take you to your destination, while mind will just try to keep you in this crazy world. Pure awareness is like gold. The intellectual mind is like brass that we try to polish to make it look like gold, even though we all have this real gold within us all the time.

We experience our nondual pure awareness once every twenty-four hours. It might be through a shock, a yawn, a surprise, or a "wow" moment. The fact that we have these glimpses shows that nondual pure awareness is already within us. We just fail to recognize it because we are distracted by something else. You will only recognize it when you get the taste of it through Dzogchen introduction. The guru is showing us something we already have; we are not looking for something new. We can recognize in glimpses through the gradual process of resting the mind in meditation, and we can recognize through an introduction from the guru. The latter is not gradual and it doesn't rely on meditation. We receive the introduction and our thoughts just merge with nondual pure awareness on the spot.

If you've never tasted a strawberry and someone gives you one to eat and tells you what it is, you will recognize the flavor next time you eat one. That is introduction. It is often explained to be like telling a poor person they have a thousand pounds of gold hidden under their floor— gold that has been there all along. We also say introduction is like a finger pointing to the moon. Do you look at the finger or do you look at the moon? Most people look at the finger, but recognition is looking at the moon. The finger that is pointing is the introduction.

Only a genuine guru can give you an introduction to your own true nature, so you need to be careful who you get it from, and in turn the guru needs to be careful who they give it to. It is a person-to-person, mouth-to-ear tradition that is guarded by protector deities. You have to choose a genuine guru, one that is recognized by a proper lineage with a deep history, and then you have to merge yourself with that guru. Some teachers will say they are giving you an introduction and formalize it with a certificate, but what they are giving you is only a title; the real introduction depends on the student's realization.

Introduction used to be whispered in secret through the copper pipes that connected the rooms in Indian monasteries prior to the eighth century. It still depends on the right moment for guru and disciple. Money can't buy Dzogchen, either; you need to be ready. At some point, the introduction will happen. You don't need to try to make it happen.

The ultimate teaching is that there is just mind. Everything that happens comes about from not recognizing mind. You are currently stuck in the relative nature of mind through grasping, labeling, and judging your experiences. You follow the mind and its millions of thoughts, grasping after past, present, and future. The absolute mind is a pause, it doesn't go toward past, present, or future.

Patrul Rinpoche, one of the great masters of Dzogchen, didn't teach for years because his students were not ready. They kept asking him for an introduction, but he wouldn't give them one. One night, he called one of his long-term students to his cave just behind Dzogchen Monastery and gave him a direct introduction. "Can you see the stars?" Patrul Rinpoche asked. "Can you hear the dogs barking?" He called these two questions his introduction. Whole Dzogchen lineages have arisen from this introduction. Introduction has nothing to do with words. Intellectual people might think, "So what? I can see stars every day." We keep adding thoughts. Dzogchen is very far from thinking. We can't use the intellectual mind to talk about Dzogchen.

Samantabhadra is the pure form of your being. The only thing missing is that you don't recognize this. When you recognize it, that is already good enough. The ground is pure, the path is pure, the result is pure.

Nothing needs to be changed. We just need to recognize through introduction. Resting is the solution to being caught in samsara's net. It looks very simple, so people think it isn't good enough, but we are not trying to learn anything—we are trying to recognize something. Once you get realization the job is complete. This is not a philosophical education. You will get no answers through thinking. You will only get answers through meditation, devotion, and introduction. This is the continuity of the lineage from the omniscient Dzogchen master Longchenpa until now. It's a direct introduction, a fast track. You need to follow the lineage, have devotion, and receive the introductions. The introductions can give you realization, and once you recognize, from then on you are just maintaining that experience.

PART 3

Modern Madness

CHAPTER 16

Integration

Samsara is never going to change, but if you
practice every day, that can change you.

LIVING IN THE MODERN WORLD

SOME PEOPLE think Buddhism is just for monks and nuns and about being vegetarian, but that is not the point at all. Buddhism is about understanding the teachings, cultivating the view, and attaining realization. Buddhist practice doesn't just entail sitting practice, doing prayers and rituals, or worshiping buddhas and great masters; we need to be able to integrate spirituality into our modern lives. That is quite a difficult task given modern life is chaotic and spirituality is simple. There is nothing wrong with modern life, but it's quite crazy, and our family, friends, neighbors, and work give rise to all kinds of problems. The question is are you going to get stressed by these problems or can you deal with them in a way that is enjoyable?

We need to live more meaningfully instead of being sucked in by the influence of others through television, streaming services, and social media. All that foolish chatter is too much. There are many great things in the modern world that we can be appreciate, but we have to use modern life for a positive purpose rather than a negative one.

The modern world has failed to maintain the ancient wisdom lineages, and their histories and all the old skills are disappearing. The precious ancient lineages of the world are dying forever and we can't protect them or restore them, nor can they guide us any longer. Instead, in place of these wisdom lineages, the modern world makes up these completely fake stories. We have to work within the context of our modern lifestyles, stresses, and emotions if we want to remain peaceful in the madness. We need to integrate view, meditation, and action into our lives, both physically and mentally, because the mind is very complicated. It does bewildering things that we think are normal but are really expressions of our own stress and confusion. If you look at it, you will see that mind is like a monkey running around breaking things and making a mess. We need to tame this monkey mind, because if we follow it, we will just drive ourselves and others crazy.

TECHNOLOGY

What does it mean to be modern? To many of us, it means having advanced technology, a more scientific point of view, and faster airplanes, faster trains, faster cars, faster internet. As modern people we have better lifestyles and better living conditions because everything has been upgraded. The downside is that we have a lot more stress because we have to maintain this technology. We don't enjoy what we do have, yet we always want more, more, more. When we can't maintain all the utilities and conveniences that support our lifestyles we just become more stressed. People in the business world think that bigger is better, but that's not necessarily true. Simpler and smaller is actually better. A lot of modern technology is completely pointless because of this and has turned into a business that supports selfish purposes. People have become self-absorbed, which isn't what scientists intended; they developed technologies that were meant to be good for the world. We are just using them in the wrong way.

We have so much support in modern life; take, for example, the internet, electricity, heaters, and air conditioners. People didn't have those things in the past; they had to suffer the heat under noisy fans, and their heaters were so hot you could almost cook on them. That's how it was when I was growing up in northern India. I boarded at a Buddhist monastery for almost fifteen years. Everybody called my room "the fridge" because it was so cold; it was made of concrete and leaked water everywhere. The window faced the wrong direction, so the room got no sun. We had to survive in those conditions. In the beginning, we had no electricity and had to use coal, which was very bad for our lungs, sometimes so bad we could hardly breathe. After a while things improved; we got electrical heaters with those coils that turn red. It was such a luxury to have one in the corner of the room near your feet. Everyone would show off their heater. After a few more years we got a better one, which was like a little box with a fan inside. It was such an upgrade, we felt completely spoiled.

Modern life in Europe, Australia, and America has reached great heights, but that hasn't made people happy. You want technology to go further—you want to go to Mars and the moon. We make a big mess on Earth and then want to go somewhere else to create another mess. Asian countries like India lack support systems and infrastructure, but people are accepting and happy there. There is such good infrastructure in the West, and it all tends to function properly. People in the West typically have access to hospitals, ambulances, roads, airports, shopping centers, and food supplies. Everything runs fairly smoothly. It would make sense for Indians to stress because nothing works there. The government is supposed to fix the infrastructure but it remains in disrepair and the people still have to pay taxes. In the West, the government fixes everything and people are still unhappy. If we compare modern life today to life even thirty or forty years ago, things have improved so much, it's incredible. Now is the time to enjoy it. Otherwise, what is the point in having it?

SOCIAL MEDIA

We are all a bit distracted by the internet, with access to tablets, phones, and so many social media apps. Some people are on their devices six or seven hours a day; it's unbelievable. Whenever I go into public areas, such as an airport, everybody is looking into these little devices, nobody is free. It wasn't like that twenty years ago. People talked to each other, connected with each other, read newspapers or magazines. I'm not saying technology is wrong, but these gadgets can pull you in and become a habit; it's become almost impossible to live without them. The modern system has created that dependency. You need a mobile phone, a bank account, your login ID and password for everything, or you are not part of this world. You become an alien without them.

It's easy to get quite confused when you follow social media or watch TV because everyone out there is lying. Whether it's from a politician, the news, the media, or an influencer, it is mostly garbage and yet we follow the garbage. What is wrong with us? We need to see things truly. Some things are good and some things are bad. Human beings are a little crazy and do all kinds of mad things. Jesus suffered from the ignorance of human beings who put him to death unnecessarily. This isn't so different from what is happening these days, where journalists are killed for telling the truth about the world. The situation might be different but the story is the same. If you tell the truth, you go to jail; if you lie, you can become a leader. That's how this world is now.

If you watch the news these days, you naturally become stressed, so don't feel compelled to watch it. In the past, the news was rather objective, but now it's information designed to influence you. It's not about reporting stories, it's about trying to make you believe something. Maybe they are telling the truth, maybe not; who knows? It is pulling us in different directions. The news will present something nice if it benefits someone, otherwise it shows something bad. The truth is hiding somewhere in there. We need to be more independent, to have our own wisdom, our own view, our own understanding. That doesn't mean we have to be against everything; we still need to be able to integrate with the business world, we just don't need to be influenced by its fake stories.

There is a lot going on in the world, but there is no point in getting stressed about it. The internet and social media keep telling us things are dangerous and no good, that we need to worry about this and that. You can't do anything about it, but you have to worry about everything.

We constantly see problems on our screens or on TV that make us worry and stressed, but we don't need to follow that worry. Sometimes you might feel the world is heading for disaster, but don't believe it; it's not true. These things offer plenty of problems but no solutions, which is very unbalanced. We really don't need to worry about everything, definitely not. Nothing is wrong.

EXTERNAL THINGS DON'T BRING PEACE

External things can't make you happy if you are not already happy. External things might make you happy for a few days, but then you get fed up with them. That's the character of the mind; it's never stable and will keep shifting all the time. That's why we need to meditate and engage in spiritual practices to train the mind. It doesn't matter what sort of place you live in; if your mind is peaceful and able to rest, everything will be completely excellent. On the other hand, you might live in a palace, but if your mind isn't calm and at rest, there will be no peace at all. This is because external things can't bring peace. They might give you temporary happiness, but something will always come along to change that. You buy the latest mobile phone, but after a few years that model has been replaced by a better one. We are never satisfied; we keep on buying the latest best thing, which keeps on changing with the latest developments and fads. If you could be satisfied, it wouldn't matter what phone you had—you would enjoy it. Even an old phone would look desirable to you.

When you are satisfied, you see your husband as a nice person or your wife as an angel. Without that attitude, you look at each other and see a demon. We can make such scary faces. We need to make ourselves look more inspiring to each other. Otherwise, even our kids will get scared when they see us coming. Parents' faces should make their children happy.

Our lives are a repetition of the same stresses. How come you don't find that boring? You find spiritual practice boring, but maybe that kind of boring is good. If you feel bored when you meditate, that's okay; you shouldn't always be looking for fun. We find boredom a bit flat and unexciting and our minds keep pushing us to do something else, but it's good to be bored, because we can learn from it. Something is boring when it stops inspiring your ego. If we can understand and accept boredom, it will open us up to seeing things more clearly. We will see we are caught in samsara's net.

Maintain Your Focus

Everyone has different thoughts, emotions, and priorities. We all have good days and bad days, but we need to learn to stop following them and creating narratives around them. When you are trying to rest the mind, why do you follow your thoughts, your emotions, and your stress? Don't take your thoughts and feelings so seriously. It's just mind, it's no big deal. We make such a big deal of our thoughts and emotions and then they make a big deal of themselves. You can't stop thoughts; sometimes they come and sometimes they don't. When they come, let them come, but don't follow them. Please, do not follow them.

Practice is about integration; we need to integrate spirituality into everyday life by dealing with each problem, each thought, each stress as it arises. We can do this by accepting whatever we have and simply enjoying that. We need to keep asking ourselves, "Where does my experience come from? Where does it stay? Where does it go?" Try to see life as it is in each moment instead of just reacting to it. Believe your heart, not your mind. The heart is closer to your wisdom but it can only guide you when mind is resting. There is nowhere to go. You have everything you need already. Who is going? We create our idea of self through thoughts, so don't take them too seriously. Life is wonderful.

There is no app to help us deal with the modern lifestyle. Everybody is busy and no one has time. The mind operates very quickly and makes such fast decisions. You need to slow your decision-making down, to sit really quietly and calm your mind before you decide anything. You should never make a decision when you are panicked because it will almost certainly be the wrong decision. If you can't calm your mind, you will just keep doing things quickly until you come to the end of your life and find it has just been one long repetition of events. Then you die and are reborn, and you do the same thing all over again. You die again, are reborn again, and you keep doing that a million times more. The Dzogchen teachings are saying, "Now is the time to wake up," because we don't want to keep repeating that cycle anymore.

Learn to Remain Calm

We are not meant to be happy all the time; that's not possible. We will be happy sometimes and sad sometimes, so there is no point in following your moods. You might think your experience is unique and only happening to you, but everybody has similar problems, so don't get stressed by them. Samsara is never going to change, but if you practice every day, that can change you. You need to minimize distractions and interfering influences to find the wisdom of the great view.

How do you rest the mind when you are angry, jealous, or upset? You haven't integrated the practice well enough yet to rest the mind all the time, so your practice is still a little bit separate from everyday life. You make a schedule: "This is the time to rest the mind, and this is the time for samsara." But if you can maintain your focus in shamatha as much as possible, you can still your mind to the point where it won't really matter what distractions arise. It's like these thoughts come from the ocean and go back to the ocean. Big waves or small waves, big thoughts or small thoughts, it just comes and it goes. It won't bother you when you can remain in stillness and see thoughts and emotions as they arise. When you see a big wave coming in, you will know to be careful.

You must have that view. Sometimes you have a lot of distractions, or maybe you feel ashamed or disturbed, or you get angry or jealous. All these thoughts come and it is useless to follow them. They will just destroy you, so there is no point. It's a waste of time. Whatever happens, just be calm and maintain that calmness. We cannot control what comes and goes. Sometimes the sea is calm, sometimes it's wild, but we can't change the sea. Our mind is like this, too. In the morning it's calm, in the afternoon it's completely wild, then in the evening it's calm again. That's just how it is; it's important not to see that as wrong, it's just part of life. The first thing is to recognize this is how the mind is, but if you don't want to be affected by your emotions, you must learn to remain calm. When you can stay calm, your mind will be meditating all the time.

INTEGRATING THE DZOGCHEN VIEW

You need to integrate what you learn so you can attain realization for yourself. The trouble is that you don't believe you can do it. You believe your mind when it says, "I'm not ready; I don't have any realization, and I need to be someone different to do that." This is why we have issues connecting to the spiritual world. Resting the mind will help you get the right view. Resting itself is not the view, but it reduces your thoughts, and in those thought-free moments, you get closer and closer to the view. We have so many thoughts, so many details to remember, so many things we should and should not do—how can we be in control of them all? It's impossible. But what is possible is to just rest the mind and have the Dzogchen view. Then you don't need to worry about the millions of thoughts and worries that arise; you don't need them.

How will you integrate the view into your daily life? Usually, our problems remain in daily life and the Dzogchen view stays on the shelf. We integrate the view into daily life through meditation. In this way, meditation becomes your legs for the journey through life. When you meditate, your actions can be completed properly, and they become easier and more fun because of the view. When your mind is stable, your view becomes strong and steady like a mountain. You don't need to analyze anything; just leave everything as it is. When you have the Dzogchen view, you have an antidote that will help you to reduce or avoid your problems, and if you keep updating the view through practice and teachings, you will keep strengthening the antidote. That is how you integrate Dzogchen into everyday life.

Dzogchen is a deep science of the mind. You are learning how the mind works, how stress works, how emotions work. You will be able to say, "Oh, I know now, I can deal with stress; I can deal with samsara; I can deal with all these problems." You will have this protection, almost like wearing armor, where you will no longer be so affected by the madness. We need to work within the context of our lifestyle, stress, and emotion in order to stop being affected by the chaos. That is integration. We have to keep practicing to attain this integration, and the number one practice is upgrading your view. To have the view, you have to stop being stressed by stress. We have enough stress. Just leave the stress as it is, that's good enough; you don't need to create any more. There is nothing wrong with modern life. The only problem is stress. We need to change our stress level.

INTEGRATING DZOGCHEN MEDITATION

When you can integrate the practice into your daily life, you will become someone who is practical, simple, and humble. We call that "resolution through the practice." You are not practicing just to get a stamp on a certificate. I did this; I studied philosophy, I graduated, I got the stamp, but the stamp did nothing for me. That stamp is just a piece of paper that you can put on a wall. I learned tens of thousands of words and definitions, but this education didn't teach me how to make a cup of tea. We learn more from doing things, and meditation is that sort of training. When you learn something, you need to apply it in action, and then you will know how to deal with problems when they arise.

Everyone needs to train in working within their community, in how to support, help, and understand each other. This is not a matter of ticking a box; you need to learn to integrate your practice in your interactions with others. Then when somebody comes to you in need, you become the right person for them. You can empathize with them to the degree that you almost merge with them; you have an intimate understanding of their experience and can almost channel yourself in your response to them so that they benefit from the integration of your practice as well. This is what we call a manager. Otherwise, you are a damager, not a manager. So many managers are damagers. They damage the whole system, they damage people, they destroy organizations. We need more managers and less damagers in the business world as well as the spiritual world, people who are really grounded and can understand each other. How are you going to become a good leader? The Dzogchen view is that the path to enlightenment is not just about something you attain; it is training in leadership. The best leaders are buddhas, because they teach others how to be leaders, too.

The real purpose of meditation is to bring calm and happiness into our everyday lives. Meditation is not doing something else while we allow all our daily problems to remain. Meditation is about focusing on whatever we are doing and enjoying every moment of it. That meditation doesn't necessarily just happen on the cushion. It starts there, but it can be done anywhere, at any time. Any kind of repetitive activity can become meditation. You can meditate when you're driving, shopping, walking, washing the dishes, or cleaning the house. Whenever you do something as much as possible, again and again, you start to do it without thinking and it just runs smoothly. Meditation is habituation like this—you make it a habit no matter what is going on. That is the definition of meditation. You just watch inwardly and rest the mind.

Dzogchen meditation is about trying to "calm the farm," as they say in Australia. We are so distracted all the time but we fool ourselves into assuming our distraction is normal. This tricky mind is always interfering, so we need to integrate the view into our lives by doing meditation. Real spirituality is about understanding who you are. Your everyday life is not who you are in reality. External appearances, along with your fears of sickness, aging, and death, are not ultimately true. There is a contradiction between what you see and the way it is. We believe things are the way we see them and assume they must be that way simply because we see them that way. Our biggest challenge is to break that habit by resting the mind.

CHAPTER 17

Dealing with Stress

Stress is pointless—that's the Dzogchen view. Dzogchen is meant to relax you, to give you freedom and comfort.

SLAVES TO MIND

WE ALL GET stressed living in the modern world. It's a tough lifestyle, and things can turn upside down or negative very quickly. We work so hard, but no one appreciates our efforts and we end up burning out. Everyone has these issues. Everything makes us feel pressured, it's just one thing after another. Examine it for yourself: Does your lifestyle actually bring you happiness or does it just bring you stress? If you are happy, then modern life makes sense, but if you just get stressed by it all, it does not. You need to learn to rest and to be more flexible about your timelines. Our schedules are intense and time goes by so quickly, so we always feel pressure. Then if we don't get the job done, we feel guilty, which makes us more stressed. The way to integrate the spiritual view into modern life is to have less stress, more happiness, and more fun.

We can't be happy if we just follow modern life because human desires are made up of temporary pleasures. We go to the movies or watch sports, we go swimming, we take a holiday; we collect these little pleasures, but they require a lot of maintenance and we get stressed by the maintenance. Buddhist teachings never said we can't enjoy things, but can you handle the stress of maintaining them? If you are stressed by maintaining your pleasure, it's unhealthy. If you are not stressed by that, you are okay, you can have all those things. However, be aware that wanting pleasurable things is usually the beginning of trouble because once attachment arises, there will be stress. Pleasure only lasts a few minutes, but attachment can last a long time. We often know something isn't good for us, but we keep doing it anyway, day after day.

We are stressed now because we have been a slave to our mind for so long. We burn out when it makes us work too hard, but our mind keeps telling us, "You must do this, you must do that, you are not good enough, blah, blah, blah . . ." It's too much. We must stop that and start saying, "No, I'm not going to be a slave to my mind. I'm the boss, not you!" We see our stress as real like this, but consider where it comes from. We always blame someone else, but it comes from our own ignorance about who we are and how we are caught in samsara's net. Understanding that will become the seat of your strength and you will grow from that basis.

SAMSARA IS NEVER GOING TO CHANGE

We need to remind ourselves that we have a lot of distractions and we get distracted very easily. Each distraction starts off a chain of thought and that leads to another chain of thought. It never ends. You need to learn to stop being pulled into that chain to begin with. This is not to judge thoughts as good or bad; we are simply trying to see how we are pulled into it all. Social media, advertising, the influence of friends and family—everybody pulls us in and we just follow along without even knowing where we are going. Things that were meant to make life easier just make it more stressful. Samsara is never going to change. We want to be happy but we choose the wrong things to get us there and end up asking, "Why am I so stressed?" The answer is simple. You made the wrong choice and chose samsara. Samsara is like sitting on the tips of needles. You will never be comfortable there.

We experience three types of stress: stress from the past, stress from the present, and stress from the future. Every day, we make up storms of stress in our mind, with thoughts like "I'm not good enough" and so on. The past is gone, so leave it there. The future hasn't yet come, so don't worry. We follow stress so much that it becomes a habit, and we feel something is missing without it. We push ourselves to the edge physically and mentally. We have too much on our schedule and end up chasing time until we have no time to breathe. We want some enjoyment, but instead we get sick, or we take a holiday and it ends up being stressful. A real holiday depends on how we see things; if you can handle your own mind, it will be like you're always living in a palace, even if you are in a pigsty.

THE ABSOLUTE VIEW

We have a relative view, which comes from mind, and we have an absolute view, which comes from resting the mind. The relative view is unreal—you see something that isn't there except as an illusion. When you rest the mind, the absolute view becomes clearer because dualistic perception is gone. We need the absolute view in the modern world. We will never be able to challenge our everyday stress without it. People think that something labeled "absolute" must be difficult, but the absolute view is the easy one. It is the relative view that's difficult because it's so complicated.

I'm not saying you should live like a yogi, forsaking the modern world along with your family, social circle, and job. That is not the point. You need to earn some money for food, shelter, and health care. These things are a requirement, but you don't need to keep working to satisfy the demands of your mind. You are never going to satisfy them anyway, because they are never going to end. We work so hard to support all the things the mind demands. This leads some people to say, "I must get away from samsaric life. I can't practice in it, there's too much stress." Another approach would be to say, "Everything is an illusion, and believing I am trapped is just another illusion." These illusions, however, seem so real to us. Meditation will help us relax and rest the mind so that we stop reacting to these things.

Stress is pointless—that's the Dzogchen view. Dzogchen is meant to relax you, to give you freedom and comfort. We need to take care of our body and energy, and we need to rest the mind a lot, because the thinking mind is like an engine. If we keep the motor running in our vehicle it will burn, and once you've burned the motor, it's dead. You need to calm the mind, switch off the engine, and service it well. Rest the mind, rest the motor. Millions of thoughts keep the motor spinning all the time.

When we establish a spiritual lifestyle, our view will change. Stress will still be there, don't get me wrong; stress will be there as long as mind is there. As long as thoughts are there, stress will be there, too. When thoughts are gone, stress will be gone, but getting rid of thoughts is very difficult for the moment. Given we are so well trained in academic thinking, we are good at developing thoughts, but they never give us any security, so we never feel comfortable or confident. We just feel doubt because we believe that everything that happens to us is real.

Don't Choose Samsara

We get stressed by having too much and we get stressed by having too little. It is best to have just a little and appreciate what you have, where you live, your family, and your environment. Whatever you have, be happy with that. It's better to have a few simple choices than too many like we have now. If you only follow modern life, you can't be happy, because you will have mostly stress. You should settle for a simple life and turn the mind inward. First, recognize every thought as it arises and then let it come, let it go. You will see that you have nothing to lose and nothing to gain; that your thoughts are thieves in an empty house. Practice like that with each problem, each worry, each fear. That's how to work with your stress and remain unaffected by this modern madness.

Stress will come, but don't follow it. Let it come, let it go. You can be doing something right and obstacles will arise to stop you. The mind will come up with crazy thoughts like, "I'm no good, I'm bad." Those thoughts will come, so be prepared for them. All these disturbances are just like bubbles on the water. They are not real. Nothing is guaranteed, it's all impermanent—and when we know this, we will be prepared and our expectations will change. You may also find it helpful to get away from everything a little every day. Take a walk and stop working so hard. If you can do things with joy, you will have a different experience of stress; it will be healthy stress. If you do have a lot of stress, you can practice some deep breathing. Breathe in, then breathe out with a long and slow "AHHH . . ." If you have lot of swirling thoughts, full of anger or jealousy, breathe out forcefully with a "PHET!" Say it as a very short, loud, and wrathful sound. This will break the chain of your thoughts.

We create stress, then we react to that stress and in turn create more stress. We just follow our thoughts to happiness or to stress or to joy or to disappointment. In doing so we are choosing complicated samsara over peace. You need to see everything as an illusion and stop getting stressed by it. Just see it as it is. Does something seem really serious? It only looks serious. All our stresses are fake. They are relative truth. Relative truth refers to things that are only pretending to be real. Everything we do is fake. It never really happened. In absolute truth, it doesn't matter who is right or wrong, it's just illusion anyway. To think "He is doing bad" is an illusion. To think "She is doing good" is an illusion. We stay free of physical and mental stress when we can stay neutral. We are talking about the view here. We have to approach it differently when it comes to our actions, where we should always be kind, genuine, and humble.

Old people in Tibet don't have a lot of stress; they accept a simple life. They trust in the Dharma and don't harbor doubts like we do. They may not know much, but they keep practicing every day. We know a lot but we don't practice and we don't have trust or devotion. The older Tibetans don't want to study; they circumambulate holy sites, they turn prayer wheels, and they trust. In the West, it seems sadly that many old people are just waiting to die. Westerners have such nice houses and plenty of food and comforts, but something is missing. What is missing is spirituality and devotion. In Tibet, people live so simply but they are happy. In the West, we have so much stress, but it doesn't come from what we have; it comes from the mind. We never have enough.

WISDOM

If we have devotion to the lineage and to absolute truth, it will cut directly through stressful situations. Devotion is central in Dzogchen, but it needs to be genuine devotion, not an artificial devotion based on belief. Devotion based on belief is not stable; it changes often, which brings more stress. You don't have to create devotion, just trust life as it is. Devotion can be destroyed by doubt and fear. When devotion dominates, doubt and fear are not possible, but if we have artificial devotion merely because we think we should, it won't work. Doubt is the biggest enemy of spiritual progress. We doubt when we don't trust absolute reality and we fear taking that leap, which results in an inability to believe. We should be led by devotion, not by the intellect, because intelligence has the tendency to panic. It gets afraid and it stresses. We think we are clever, but we are not, because we do not know what is beyond this world. Mind will always tell us, "I know," but it doesn't know, and that makes us afraid.

Intellectual devotion is artificial and very unstable. You might trust someone, but because the mind changes so easily, after twenty years you have become enemies. Real devotion comes spontaneously. It's not created by mind, it's already born within you. If you have that devotion, you don't need anything else; everything will come from that. Just go back to your buddha nature and remain at rest there. You don't need to create devotion, nor do you need to strive to increase it, just maintain it and devotion will grow by itself. This is the blessing of the lineage, of the buddhas, of Guru Rinpoche. Trust the Buddha, trust Guru Rinpoche, and don't follow your monkey mind. If you do that, your suffering and stress will be fun—it will become a teaching, a method to grow and expand.

Recognize your thoughts, learn to relax, and remain calm. Let come, let go. That's how we gain wisdom. If you think something is a problem, you will get stressed and wisdom won't come, so give your thoughts some space. We can't do two things at the same time. We are either in samsara or we are not. Real Dzogchen practitioners are so happy, they are never stressed. The Dzogchen view has no room for stress. We are not interested in pretending to be happy; we want genuine happiness. Can you taste the flavor of that happiness? You have everything you need. You have this incredible true nature. Whenever I introduce this Dzogchen lineage, I always explain that you don't need to become better, you are already good enough. The only thing you need to do is recognize. That's it. You already know, but you miss it because your mind is frozen. You need to defrost it. It is time to melt your mind.

CHAPTER 18

Follow Your Heart

There is something more inside us, inside our heart,
beyond the physical. What is the heart? It is our true nature.

COMMON SENSE

WE ARE ALL looking for happiness in the wrong direction. Turn your mind inward instead. You will see who you are: how wild the mind is when it's distracted, and how incredible the mind is when it's at rest. When mind is distracted, we call it "mind." When we rest the mind, we call that "heart." We should follow our heart because the heart is constant and reliable. You can trust it. Resting the mind creates a gap for the heart to lead. Meditation is about keeping three things together: your body, mind, and energy. We use shamatha to calm the body and settle the mind so that our common sense can guide us. When the heart leads, you start to experience life completely differently. You will have a better view, greater confidence, and less doubt because the heart is pure, spontaneous wisdom.

Normally, we are never guided by our common sense. Instead, we are guided by the negative emotions and by the worry and fear that are created by television, social media, and politics. When we look at the situations of current events in the world, they all seem quite scary, and there is something wrong everywhere we look. That is how we let ourselves be tricked into being guided by worry and fear. Except worry and fear are completely useless. We have everything we need: we have this incredible power called common sense, which comes from the heart. When we worry and watch out for ourselves in fear, we have a little chicken heart. We need to have a big heart. We need to trust, to be generous, to listen to our heart and give it the opportunity to lead instead of letting our intellect constantly interfere. If you don't create space for the heart to lead, you will always be led by mind, and your mind won't let you free. Mind will keep telling you to trust it, but when mind is in control, common sense never gets the chance to lead.

THE TRICKY MIND

We are completely influenced by this artificial mind. It tells us to do something and we just follow whatever it says. It makes us panic, it spins out millions of thoughts, and we make the wrong decisions. The mind hides behind you without showing its face. It says, "I'm not responsible for what you do," but it guides everything in your life. We pretend our mind is not tricky, but we know it is. When we follow the mind, we blame our stress on each other. Spouses blame spouses, friends blame friends, kids blame each other. Ask yourself: "Do I want to be a slave to my mind or be led by my wisdom?" The heart has no trickiness, it is very transparent. We must decide not to be fooled by this tricky mind anymore.

We are often afraid to follow our heart. We think people will take advantage of us if we do, so we keep following the mind because it seems safer. Following the mind is our strongest habit. The influence of the mind is so strong; we fear losing, we fear change, we even fear enlightenment. Mind doesn't believe things can change; its nature is doubt. We have to accept that samsara is difficult and adjust to it where we can, but we also need to understand that mind is always leading us and it leaves no space for the heart. Mind is like a monkey in a cage, it just keeps jumping all over the place. This crazy monkey mind is a dangerous thing, because it just pops up and dominates everything so quickly, we don't even notice it. When you do happen to notice, you think, "Wow, how did that happen?" It has just taken charge so quickly.

Mind is high maintenance, but following your heart is low maintenance. We don't have family wisdom lineages anymore, where specific cultural knowledge is maintained in families and communities, which is why we are a little lost, and we just assume we can trust ourselves. But can you really trust yourself? You have so many thoughts coming and going, both good and bad, so be honest about this. You are not perfect. You have negative thoughts, and that's okay. The trick is to maintain a calm and peaceful mind throughout, but we find that very difficult to do. It is so difficult for us because we have been with our friend the mind for too long. Your mind is not a good friend to you. It is a very tricky friend. Your heart is your best friend. You can trust your heart, but you don't follow it. If you have done your best from your heart, there will always be a good return. If you have responded from your tricky mind, you will get a bad return. That is the nature of samsara.

The heart is kind and flexible, while the mind is rigid and tricky, so it's difficult for them to be friends. Mind is so fickle and manipulative, it showers us in thoughts, but mind is baseless—you cannot find it under examination. It is hard to trust and be friends with your mind because mind loves drama. Without drama, mind gets bored, so we need a lot of distractions to keep the mind entertained. Mind gets easily disturbed by other people with tricky minds, but the heart is not disturbed by that. Heart is the best friend for the heart and it is also good for the mind. Heart is friends with everybody. Mind is very lucky to have a heart. Heart is unlucky to have a mind.

THE EGO PLATFORM

In Dzogchen, the mind has two platforms: an ego platform and a wisdom platform. When the ego is leading, all the thoughts of the three times are present. When wisdom is leading, there are no thoughts. When you rest your mind in the gap, your inner wisdom can guide you. You are in the right spot. But you never give wisdom this opportunity. You have wisdom but you never use it, because the intellect is always interfering.

Mind always needs to promote the comfort zone of the ego. The ego is never comfortable. Sometimes it even makes you sick or weak, or it says you are not good enough, telling you that you have this problem and that problem, leading you to think there is always something missing. Mind is constantly saying, "You must worry; be careful, you might get sick or die." Mind is the thief that comes to steal your peace. It's always looking for an opportunity to undermine you. That is the narrative of the ego, not anyone else, and none of it is true. You are not sick, you are good enough, you have everything you need. The only thing you lack is recognition. To recognize, you must rest the mind, which requires the constant practice of mindfulness. You need to rest in the gap and stay on track, even when fears, doubts, and worries arise. Rest the mind and try not to follow your intellect.

Ego belongs to the intellectual mind, and intelligence is always trying to protect you or to save you. It does that even if you don't need protection. Intelligence judges, and it's very clever, trying to protect your secrets and hide your weaknesses. We have a constant fear of being attacked and feel we need to protect ourselves. Some people love the ego, especially in the business world, where a bigger ego equals more success. In the spiritual world it is the opposite, but people also have egos in the spiritual world; they still love titles and power. We should understand that in whatever world we find ourselves, ego is painful, and we torture ourselves when we maintain its influence. We should all work from the heart, but ego gets in the way.

In Dzogchen, all of that doesn't matter; we just relax and follow our heart. You are who you are, and praise or blame won't change that. In the business world, people must have the best of everything, the best clothes, the best possessions, the best reputation. The Dzogchen teachings say we should just enjoy what we've got. Our intelligence is creating samsara, and if we follow our intellect, we will always be at war, wanting this, not wanting that. We will debate, we will fight, we will get depressed and feel anxious—but there is nobody there to experience all of this, we have just created these problems by following the tricky mind. We need to look deeper than this intelligence. Go to the heart, recognize its stability and power, and start to follow that instead. It is incredible. There are two kinds of magic. We are currently in the magic of ignorance, but we are discovering another magic, another part of ourselves.

THE WISDOM PLATFORM

We talk about right view and wrong view in Buddhism. In Dzogchen, right view is to act genuinely from the heart, which is without expectations. Wrong view is to act from the intellect, which is loaded with agendas and expectations. Do the right thing from your heart, which is the wisdom platform. Even if other people don't see your motivation or acknowledge your hard work, it doesn't matter; just do your best without thinking, "I'm being good, I want to make someone happy." It's good to have the motivation to do your best. If you can't, however, you shouldn't get stressed by that either. Just accept that it wasn't possible.

Start by knowing who you are. Are you genuinely calm? Are you being tricky? Look inward and see if you are following the monkey mind or the heart. If you are following the monkey mind, you will go up and down quite quickly. You will find you try to prove to others that you are a nice person. If you really are a nice person, is it necessary to prove that to anyone? If you are looking for proof, you are acting from your ego. People love to be "somebody." Everyone knows we make a big deal of ourselves, especially our position and power in society. We make our lives so stressful sustaining this "I." It is so high maintenance. We think we know better than others, when we should be humble and listen to others.

Stress will come, but don't follow it. Just let come, let go. You can be doing something right and obstacles will come up to stop you, or your crazy mind will take over with thoughts of "I'm no good." Other times we feel like we want to be heard, or if someone hurts us, we want to challenge them. Those thoughts will come, so be prepared for them. Understand all of that is the weakness of the intellect. If you practice Dzogchen, you will understand that you don't need to do any of those things the mind tells you to do. You can just be yourself and no one can harm you.

The real solution to these things is to have trust and devotion, as well as compassion and kindness. These are the most powerful antidotes to all the problems and obstacles in our lives. They are good enough on their own, but we usually don't trust that. We think we need to *do* something. We believe our own ideas and don't see the reality of cause and effect. Ask yourself, "Am I happy?" The heart will always say, "I'm happy," and the mind will always say, "I'm not happy." Mind is an attention seeker. Heart is content with whatever.

Mind is like a puppet master making us dance. But we don't have to let it lead us. Follow the heart instead. Everybody's mind is tricky but the heart is not part of that club, it always tells you the truth. It's genuine and honest. When you follow the heart, you will have more wisdom. Our inner wisdom is clarity; it is beginningless purity. We call that Kuntuzangpo in Tibetan, or Samantabhadra in Sanskrit, the "always good," because we are pure from the beginning. That is who we are, but we find it hard to accept that.

Devotion is one of the keys for opening the door to enlightenment. Resting the mind is devotion. Keeping the guru in your heart is devotion. These all help you to recognize your true nature. When you keep devotion in your heart, the guru and the lineage are alive and your realizations will definitely increase. Devotion is a complicated subject in the modern world. We can't trust anything these days, but we need to trust. Unconditional trust in someone is very difficult for us because the person doesn't seem perfect. No one is perfect, but we keep looking for perfection. You need to trust the path and have devotion in the guru. If you want someone to be perfect, you need to ask what "perfect" is for you. You will find it's an illusion. You need to see life just as it is.

You don't want to believe that enlightenment is close. Your mind says, "No, you are not ready for enlightenment, don't go there." But enlightenment is right here. It's always with you. You are searching for it outside but nobody has ever found it there. You need to know the secret of the mind: the mind is hiding your true nature within itself. If you trust your mind, you have a bad friend that won't take you anywhere. If you trust your heart, you will find enlightenment. So follow your heart and not your mind. There is something more inside us, inside our heart, beyond the physical. What is the heart? It is our true nature. Pure awareness is in the heart. If you don't recognize your true nature, your mind will take your pure awareness to hell. Who is your best friend? Your pure awareness. You have to stay away from your bad friend, the mind, and stay with your pure awareness as much as possible, then you will be safe.

There is nowhere else to be but here. Where is "here"? We are like the farmer out searching for his cow in the forest when the cow is at home in the shed, happy and healthy and eating grass. The shed symbolizes the heart, because your happiness and peace are already with you. You don't need to go anywhere. It's enough to be present wherever you are. When you are heart-centered, your buddha nature is already there. To really follow the heart you need to rest the mind completely. When your mind is calm, you create a gap and give the heart a chance to lead. Don't trust your dangerous friend, the mind. Just practice resting the mind. That is how you open your heart.

CHAPTER 19

Acceptance

Whenever you are stressed, stop and ask yourself,
"What can I do?" You can accept it.
Sometimes acceptance is a solution.

MIND IS NEVER SATISFIED

WE ALL GET stressed by other people, and that is the nature of samsara. We just need to relax and learn to accommodate people. When you are happy, notice it and enjoy it. When you are sad, notice it and accept it. Don't try to change these feelings or your mind will become your master, you will keep following it and trying to either change, reject, or adjust your circumstances. The intellectual mind is all about drama and stories, and we are usually dominated with these thoughts. We think we can handle ourselves, but we can't, and it's disastrous when we try. We need to take a more spiritual approach, one in which we can, for example, see fear without experiencing it as fear. The mind is like a big screen with a movie projected onto it—and we just keep watching the story and believing it to be true.

Human beings are guaranteed to have four kinds of suffering: birth, old age, sickness, and death. We have no choice about them; if we are born, death is inevitable. Everything is conditional and we have to accept that. If we can relax and accept what comes, negative situations will slowly turn into positive ones. When things are difficult or they are not working out for you, just accept it; don't go into deep samsara. You can still get angry and tired and stressed sometimes, because as long as we have a mind and a body, stress will be there to some extent.

ACCEPTANCE IS A SOLUTION

People worry because they don't know what's going to happen in the future. They blame each other for their problems, too. There are so many fake stories circulating, but you don't need to believe them; just be positive, enjoy things, and don't add to other people's fears. Some Buddhists say we should live simply and give up our possessions, but for many of us that's just another kind of ego trip. There is no point in showing off how simple you are. You need to *be* simple, not *show* simple. You need to *be* respect, too, because showing respect is also fake. We should learn to be satisfied, to set limits on ourselves and accept what we have. Otherwise, we will have everything we need and still become stressed because of the mind's demands. The mind is never satisfied. It's like how some people, when you give them an inch, they take a mile. You need to say to yourself, "I will accept whatever I have and be happy with that." You can have more, that's no big deal—but it doesn't serve you to be greedy about it. Whenever you are stressed, stop and ask yourself, "What can I do?" You can accept it. Sometimes acceptance is a solution.

Once you accept something, it becomes easier. If you can change it, you should change it. But if you have no choice, then accept it. There is no point in getting upset in the process. Try your best in life, but if it doesn't work out in your favor or you make a mistake, simply regret it, accept it, and move on. When we accept the challenges and disappointments of life, we don't suffer. When we resist these things, life can be genuinely difficult. This is not to say you should accept any bullying, manipulation, and aggression. But in other circumstances, you need to accept and appreciate what you do have and where you live, as well as your overall situation, your family, and your environment. Sometimes feelings are very disturbing and it's hard to accept them. When Tibetans lost their country, they didn't wallow; they saw it as their karma. They thought it was best to practice their culture and do good things so maybe they could reverse that karma. Are they happy? Maybe not, but by taking responsibility in that way, they can accept the loss. Accepting the situation makes a big difference. It's such a powerful tool.

SPONTANEOUS ACCEPTANCE

You can't buy buddha nature and you can't share your own buddha nature, either. It has always belonged to you. The way to discover your buddha nature is by accepting it. There are two ways to accept something: there is intellectual acceptance and spontaneous acceptance. Spontaneous acceptance is quite different, but it's difficult, because we tend to only be willing to accept something if we know it's safe. We always have terms and conditions, because it is a challenge to drop our fears and enter the unknown. Intellectual acceptance is artificial, however, because you "believe" you have a true nature, but who is actually there to believe? It's the mind that believes. Forget mind. Your true nature is there. It has always been there. And you already have everything you need.

In Dzogchen, trust means to see everything as it is and accept that. You don't need to see anything as "good" or "bad," just see it as it is and leave it as it is. That is trust. You trust the way it is. You know your friend might be nice in the morning and grumpy in the afternoon because everything is based on impermanence. Knowing this, you won't be surprised when things change. Friends become enemies. No big deal. This trust is quite simple because you know what you see, and you don't expect anything else.

Everything we experience is completely manipulated by mind. We need to avoid samsaric distractions and learn to accept things, or the mind will never be satisfied. If you follow your mind, it will be impossible for you to be simple and easygoing. If you don't follow your mind, everything will be possible. You need acceptance in this way because you need to come back from being lost. You don't believe you are a buddha, you believe you are a human being, a nobody who has to become a somebody. Accept who you are, as it is. This is a very deep Dzogchen view. Acceptance is trust. Do you trust who you are? Do you trust your view? Do you trust your future? Accepting with the mind is good, but it's easier to accept with the heart. The mind wants all kinds of terms and conditions. The heart is quite easygoing.

THE CHOICE OF NO CHOICE

We can follow our emotions and become part of the business world or we can stop following our emotions and follow a spiritual path. We also have a third choice, the "choice of no choice" that is Dzogchen. When you have no choice, you accept what you have, which is the best choice of all. Sometimes we feel we have to fight for things, but why fight? You can't make everyone happy. Samsara will never be a great place to be. Just accept that. In samsara it is guaranteed we will have health issues, we'll age, and someday we'll die. We don't want to get old, but what choice do we have? That is the choice of no choice.

In Dzogchen, we don't want to be perfect; we would rather be honest. Ego maintains our profile and identity by protecting itself, but we can't hide our weaknesses forever. Samsara is a big mess. We live in the mess and we have to accept it, but we don't want samsara to damage us. So just let come, let go. One day you will die and lose everything, so you must be ready for that. It's important to develop flexibility now because a strong habit of attachment to things will make sure you get stuck in samsara forever. Learn to accept who you are. You are a good and kind person. If someone says otherwise, it's not true. Trust yourself. If you feel sad and tired, that's fine—that's life. You need to learn to integrate and accept your lifestyle, instead of always being unhappy with something and losing time being distracted by all the drama.

If something is impossible, accept that and let go. Don't try to make it possible. Its best to develop your view so you don't get stressed by all this samsaric drama. You can want a different life but you really have no choice, so just accept the life you have. Then no choice becomes a choice. You can enjoy every moment, appreciate what you have, and be happy with that. You can't always be happy, that's not possible, but there's nothing wrong with that. That's the samsaric lifestyle and those are its conditions.

Whether you live in a palace or have no home, learn how to integrate your lifestyle and accept that life is not against you. We are always challenging life, never happy with this or that. This causes so much trouble for us and we never get to enjoy it. We waste time getting unnecessarily distracted by all this drama. Stop the drama, enjoy your life, and be helpful and kind to each other. Then, when death comes, you will be able to say, "I made the most of my time, now I can die peacefully." If you can't accept the circumstances of your life you will feel guilty and think, "I was selfish and arrogant; I've done nothing."

Happiness will still come and go, but that is no problem when you can accept sadness as well as happiness. Whatever comes, no one will be able to upset your balance. When you stop trying to change sadness into happiness and just accept whatever comes, you will have peace. Let go and stop taking yourself so seriously. If you are peaceful and your house is peaceful, other people will be able to feel that energy. Take this practice of acceptance into your everyday life and stop reacting to whatever is before you.

CHAPTER 20

Finding Balance

We become emotionally imbalanced when
what we are doing is all about ourselves. It's better
for us if we learn to be "clever-selfish."

MAINTAIN A STABLE BASE

AS HUMAN BEINGS, we are overly attached to our thoughts and feelings, grasping onto them all the time. These feelings don't really help us. They lead every which way, making us happy one moment or sad the next. We are influenced by friends, family, partners, neighbors, grandparents, and grandkids; everyone tries to sway us, saying, "This is good for you, this is bad for you," and we just listen. This makes our lives difficult and we become mentally imbalanced. It may seem like you have no control over such influences, but thinking that way only gives the mind too much power. You need to stop doing that.

How do you deal with your emotional disturbances? Do you stay in deep samsara and take it out on others? We have such a strong tendency to think, "I'm right, you're wrong. I'm always right!" The ego finds it hard to accept being wrong. An alternative to thinking about who is right or wrong is to rest the mind. That will remove the need to either blame someone else or to defend yourself. Resting the mind is the middle way between right and wrong. Whenever you get emotionally upset, don't make a big deal of it—just breathe in, breathe out, and let it go.

We need to find stability through meditation; that is the only way to maintain a balanced and stable state. Emotions aren't necessarily bad, but they can be extremely powerful, so we need to know how to calm them. The energy of our thoughts and emotions can build until we feel like a pressure cooker about to blow. You need to calm those emotions— all those tigers and snakes, don't wake them up! Learn to rest your mind as much as possible. Doctors diagnose so many problems with our health and they recommend so many restrictions, but they don't often acknowledge how imbalanced emotions are the causes of disease. You have to recognize your monkey mind. If you bring the monkey into your house, it will break everything.

Handling Your Emotions

The goal is not to get rid of emotions, rather to learn how to handle them. We need to learn to balance; it's always a balance. Sometimes people deliberately try to push you off-balance. If they are really upset and their emotions are out of balance, they will try to make you upset, too. They just add fuel to the fire. A friend might come to you crying and make you cry, too; or they might be angry and try to make you angry so that you both get upset. That's how we usually behave when our emotions are out of balance.

Strong emotions can't always be prevented. The nature of fire is hot, the nature of ice is cold, and the nature of anger is to fire up. How should we deal with emotions like anger? There is nothing wrong with anger itself, the problems come from how we add to it, how we exaggerate and conceptualize it. That's what makes our emotions so toxic. Each thought conditions your emotions and moods, each thought creates worry, sadness, and fear; thoughts never let you rest. You just need to recognize this without making a big deal of it. Tomorrow it will change. When you react to a situation by being upset, your intellectual mind is happy, since it's the role of the intellect to make you upset. Mind says, "I've done my job." Heart says, "No, there's nothing to be upset about. I create my own problems, nobody else is doing it." Other people may add fuel to the flames but the fire is yours.

If someone is angry in your family or workplace and you respond with anger, the situation can become explosive. That's how the everyday world operates. We try to take revenge, but it spirals out of control. If you take revenge, and they take revenge, it will never end. So don't take revenge, just leave it, ignore it, forget it. When someone else is very upset, it's important for you to remain calm, because your calmness can help that person become calm. It might not happen immediately, but if you don't respond, it amounts to the same thing.

That's how the tricky mind works. People always do something and then wait for a reply. If you give them an answer, you are asking for trouble. Just think to yourself, "Oh, this is going to be trouble, just walk away," and they will get fed up and leave you alone. It's important to see life as it is. If you are cooking on a hot stove, you will burn your finger if you touch it, so you turn the stove off and wait for it to cool down. You must understand the nature of the other person. If they are very angry, you can't touch them or things will only get worse. You need to give that person some space, some gap, until it's okay to reach out again.

CLEVER-SELFISH

You can have positive emotions where you try to be helpful to others if you genuinely want to give them support, but if you are waiting to feel happy before you help someone or waiting to feel better because you helped them, that's just about meeting your own desires. When you help someone, you will get a lot of stress, no doubt, but that is a sign you are really doing something. Whether you accept that stress or not is another story. If you help others, you will have a more enjoyable life. If you isolate yourself and become very individualistic, you will be excluded by genuine people and only accepted by a community that is a little tricky. Human beings are not stupid, they can see, no matter what they do. If you really want to help someone, you must completely dissolve the "I" and "want." Then if someone doesn't appreciate your help, it doesn't matter. You did your best from the heart.

If your ego is controlling you, you can't help anyone; forget it. You will always be saying, "I'm trying my best, but they are no good, they don't see what I'm doing." You think "I" is there, helping, but where is your "I"? If you examine your "I," you can't find it. Yet if you don't examine it, it pops up. That's how it is. If you want to help someone, don't say "I" am here to help "you." Not at all.

We become emotionally imbalanced when what we are doing is all about ourselves. It's better for us if we learn to be "clever-selfish." We are clever-selfish when we help others because this is the best way to help ourselves. You will feel joy and genuinely connect with people, and you won't feel lonely or isolated. You will find balance within yourself and balance within your community. Problems will still arise, because there are a lot of fake people in the world and they will be unhappy when you are not fake. Fake people are good friends with each other and genuine people are good friends with each other. Fake people only care about their image and reputation, their own pleasure and happiness. Everything gets completely out of balance when the focus is always "me, me, me."

A LIGHT TOUCH

We need to have a different view at the level of Dzogchen, a different kind of strategy when we approach our lives. We normally stress and say, "This is bad karma, this is good karma; this is a bad action, this is a good action," and make a big deal of it. Dzogchen is about turning the mind inward and constantly watching these rampant emotions and thoughts. We need to figure out what to do with them, since they will just keep coming. Emotions aren't necessarily good or bad, but it's important to ask yourself, "Are they helping me or not?" That is the real question. If these feelings have been ruining your relationships, destroying your happiness, and spoiling everything around you, they are not helpful.

You need to become familiar with yourself. Are you calm or are you tricky? Do you follow the monkey mind? Are you trying to prove you are nice? It is not necessary to prove you are nice, it's enough to *be* nice. You can be nice, you can be nasty, you can be competitive, you can be protective of yourself. If we accept unhappiness as part of life, it won't bother us too much. When good feelings come; recognize them and don't get attached. If we have this light touch about our feelings, it won't matter what other people do. We need to understand the way human beings are. They are friends in the morning, enemies in the afternoon, and friends again the next day. That's true for everyone, that's life, so instead of avoiding your feelings, just accept them.

Even buddhas have emotions, but buddhas don't get distracted by them, while you follow them all the time. You need to be able to recognize your powerful emotions. Anger, for example, is very dangerous; it can instantly destroy all the good karma you have built up over a long time. Anger comes from having the wrong view, so you must recognize it immediately and understand its danger. You have experienced it many times before, so say, "Yes, my old friend, I know you very well." It's like meeting up with a friend from the past. You know he likes coffee, not tea. She likes wine, not whiskey. You know how to handle the meeting. We must do the same thing with our negative emotions. When you recognize emotions as old friends, none of them will harm you. You can stand back and acknowledge them without getting sucked in.

We are not trying to control our emotional reactions, we only need to learn to identify them and let them go as soon as they arise. If you light the fuse on a firecracker there will be an explosion, but if you hold a firecracker in your hand without lighting it, there won't be any consequences. You have to be prepared for the dangers that come with following your emotions. Jealousy, doubt, fear, anger and desire will all come back; you have lived with them for too long and become too comfortable with them. They are almost like your best friends.

Meditation is about training the mind to bring balance to your emotions. You can't get rid of them, they are always there, but you can balance them whenever they arise. When you learn to swim, you need to know how to float to stay above water. We also need to know how to float above our emotions. We are not judging emotions as right or wrong, this is about finding balance. Everybody has anger, jealousy, pride, and attachment, but if you can find that balance, they won't harm you. That's why meditation is so important. Dzogchen is about balancing and integrating your emotions so they no longer affect you. When you can watch your emotions come and go, you will be able to see them as the drama of the mind.

WISDOM AND EMOTION

Mind and wisdom are two roots that give rise to two kinds of emotions. One is independent and free and the other is quite sticky. Someone might offer you a cup of coffee in a genuine way and you can drink it quite well. Someone else might offer it wanting something in return, which isn't genuine and will make the coffee hard to swallow. Expectations can destroy everything. The sticky feelings come from jealousy, anger, attachment, and greed, and they disturb everybody. We disturb each other, which is very silly, but we do it all the time.

The emotions that come from wisdom include trust, devotion, stability, and power because they all come from the energy of emptiness. Trust and devotion are especially important in Dzogchen. We just need to recognize our own incredible devotion, but our habit is to shut it away and try to develop an artificial devotion. Artificial devotion is not genuine, so you can't maintain it. You don't need to do that; it's not a requirement to manufacture devotion. The problem is you don't recognize the devotion that you have, which is already perfect. Your emotions can have an impact also, you can get upset and block your devotion, but devotion and buddha nature are within you all the time.

You should understand where you are, what you have, and what is missing. Maybe nothing is missing. We all have what we need for enlightenment but we don't recognize it and keep looking for it elsewhere. Wherever you go, just watch your mind. Don't think you are going to miss out on something, that you are going to lose something or that you need to achieve something. That is how the human mind operates. Just relax and calm yourself. Everything you need will come by itself. You don't need to worry about it.

CHAPTER 21

Breaking Habits

We need to break our old "pick and choose" habit
and change it to a "let come, let go" habit.

Hidden Habits

A CORE ASPECT OF Buddhism is avoiding bad habits and developing good habits. In Dzogchen we want to get rid of all habits, but right now, we have many bad habits and we need to do something about that first. We lie, we drink too much alcohol and coffee, we eat too many sweets. Maybe these things are okay in moderation, but if we let them take over, they will just lock us into samsara and destroy our inner peace. Many of our habits are introduced by our communities and countries, our different cultures, customs, and lifestyles. Those habits lead us to make different choices about what we like or do not like. Because we are born into a particular culture we are happy with some things and unhappy with others. Some habits are good, some habits are bad, some habits are neutral. Indians who immigrate to Australia crave hot curry because they have that habit. We eat three meals a day out of habit. Letting go of our habits is not easy, but it is possible.

The difficulty arises when a habit comes with a strong attachment to our own views. We get locked into certain ideas out of habit. If we have doubts and insecurities, we create an uncertain reality and then follow that reality. The mind is comparable to pure water in a bucket. The water is clear, but if you drop some colored dye into the bucket, the whole contents will turn that color. We are colored by our experiences all the time. We change the color constantly and our likes and dislikes keep changing according to that. Modern life is a color. Spirituality is a method for keeping the water clear and pure, but we are already stained by so many colors, we need to purify our minds by removing our habits and habitual thought patterns.

There is no point in trying to cover up our negative emotions; it's better to see the truth. Expecting to always be happy is a fairy tale. The underlying problem is that we hide our habits. We keep our hidden faults secret and don't want others to see them. We feel guilty if others see our weakness. And we think, "I'm not good enough." We hide our negative habitual thoughts and emotions but sometimes they arise strongly and other people see our true colors. It's important to be honest and to stop hiding our faults and trying to present a good front to others. We don't always have to protect our hurt feelings. Our problems have nothing to do with who we are, they are just habits, but we don't think we can change. That is not true. We need to admit things, we can't just keep hiding from them. We will pay a karmic price if we do. There is a Tibetan saying, "Your life and your karma go together like a bird and its shadow." When a bird is flying high in the sky, we might not see its shadow on the ground, but when it comes down to land, its shadow is always there to meet it. We likewise may not see the karma we are creating but when the time comes for it to ripen, the consequences of our actions are just as unavoidable.

RIGHT VIEW

People often come to enjoy their negative habits. Even though the habit is stressful, they like it, it's become part of their routine. It can be quite dangerous, however, if emotional stress becomes a habit. You feel you need to maintain the continuity of stress because you thrive on it, because you need it to feel alive. It will be beneficial for you to stop this kind of habitual stress in your daily routine. Otherwise, the habit will keep trying to maintain the stress, and you will think you can't help it even though you can. You just don't want to stop because the habit is controlling your mind. Children want to eat sweets all the time. They will destroy their teeth and ruin their health if we let them, but they don't like being disciplined. People don't like boundaries. We are also like this with ourselves. We don't try to tame our negative habits even though they might destroy us. We should reflect on our own experience and watch what the mind is doing instead of being stubborn and refusing to change.

Some bad habits go back to parental abuse. That is the transmission, the initiation, the behavior that creates a lineage of its own. Our thoughts get associated with the strong emotions of childhood trauma and they become an emotional or mental scar. The trauma itself is gone, but the scaring has become a habit. In the same way that a grain of rice is covered with skin that must be removed for us to be able to eat it, our traumatic experiences get covered by our habitual responses, and we must get rid of that skin of habit by cutting through the intellectual responses we have created.

Habits are like a drop of oil on a piece of paper; it's hard to clean it out, the oil gets in so deep. We all develop different habits from television, movies, magazines, politics, and social media. They shape our views and our views give rise to the habits and actions that we follow. We live in modern madness, which lacks both wisdom and common sense. We need to develop the right view so that the madness stops influencing us and we can challenge it. We are currently led by our habits—we like this, we don't like that—but having the right view will stop those habits from leading us. Our right or wrong habits depend on our view.

Old Socks

There's a joke that illustrates the way we continue to bring along our old habits even when we think we have changed. In early times, the Indian prime minister and his foreign minister were invited to England to meet and dine with the Queen and British politicians. The prime minister sat next to his foreign minister and began to feel uneasy, because his foreign minister's socks were very smelly. He thought, "We are representing the biggest democratic country in the world. This won't do." He gave his foreign minister some money to buy a new pair of socks. At the next meeting the foreign minister still gave off a bad odor. The prime minister was embarrassed and asked, "Did you buy the new socks like I asked you to?" The foreign minister replied, "Oh yes, I bought the new socks. I'm wearing them now. Here look, I have the old socks in my pocket to prove it!"

This is what we sometimes do. We no longer need our old habits, but we bring them along to prove we have changed. Why do you need to prove that? Just do your best. That is good enough. When you try to prove something, you spoil it and you undo all your good work. You are not supposed to prove acts of compassion or kindness. You just do it and let go. If you need a certificate or special recognition for your positive actions, any merit from that act will disappear. If you don't get any recognition, your merit will stay intact. We need our merit bank to be full, but this doesn't mean we need to have our experience confirmed as authentic by someone else.

We always bring the mind along, and it sticks its nose in everywhere. Mind is always trying to prove it has changed. When you are resting the mind, you don't need to bring your intellect anymore. That is just like holding onto your old socks. We need to keep the mind completely clear and without thought, and just remain like that. Don't bring your old socks to prove you have new socks, and don't bring your intellectual ideas to label your experiences.

Most of the time we are habitually distracted by samsara, minute after minute. Meditation is how we change this habit. We need to see our habitual thought patterns, the ones that return again and again, and learn to recognize them as they arise. We need to break the habit of believing in the relative, intellectual mind. Intelligence is a part of the mind that needs to be liberated. The intellect makes moral judgments of good and bad, right and wrong, and we make such a big deal of it. We are quite stubborn in the wrong way. We are stubborn about the wrong view when we should be stubborn about the right view. When you have right view, your habits will not lead you. Right view can see when something is a habit. We are trying to build the new habit of calming ourselves so we can see negativity when it arises. That's why our view is so important and why we need to develop the good habit of meditation.

BEYOND KARMA

When you want to cross a river, you should start swimming a fair distance upstream, so that you reach the other side at your intended location with the help of the current. The current will not let you swim straight across and you don't want to end up somewhere downstream. In our lives, too, we should stop trying to swim against the current. In the relative system, we try to go against the current, which makes life difficult because we are fighting against karma. We all want to challenge our karma, but that is impossible. Karma is built for us. People in business and political systems think they can dominate the world, but no one can dominate the karmic system. We must let go of "I" and "want." Where there is an "I" there is a strong ethos of "my way or the highway," and we'll fight with each other to get our way. Thinking like this is fighting against the karmic system. It's like trying to swim upstream in a fast current. You can't do it.

We shouldn't take good and bad too seriously, but at the same time we must respect karma, understanding that positive actions lead to positive results and negative actions lead to negative results. Karma makes everything function—our work, health, relationships, successes, and obstacles. Developing a meditation practice is cultivating a positive habit. Dzogchen is not trying to discourage bad thoughts and encourage good thoughts; it's about transcending both good and bad thoughts. Dzogchen believes in karma, but karma only operates when we follow our thoughts. When mind is resting there is no karma.

Who made you believe you are not buddha? Your mind. Your habitual mind makes you feel you aren't enlightened, and you believe it when it tells you, "You are not a buddha, you are flawed!" That is just the pillow talk of the mind. We have to break that habit. You are good enough; you have everything you need. If you stay too long with your mind, you will stink like your mind, just as a tomato that's kept with an onion will start to smell like the onion. Spend more time with the nondual pure awareness of rigpa. We need to break our old "pick and choose" habit and change it to a "let come, let go" habit. Karma is an apparition and Dzogchen is beyond it. When we escape samsara, we carry our wisdom and go beyond karma. We access Dzogchen through trust. You need to have a kind of blind trust. You don't need to have a reason for it. In this context, blind trust is genuine trust. Currently, you trust your own mind, but you need to develop a new trust; you need to trust who you are. Meditation helps you to destroy the wrong view of yourself because it breaks the habit of seeing things through your belief systems and habits. When you disempower the mind in meditation, your habits will start to dissolve by themselves.

CHAPTER 22

Relationships

*Try not to add to your stress by refusing to accept
the conditioned nature of relationships. That's life.
It's just a process of learning.*

Modern Life

WE HAVE so much trouble in the modern world because it's not really supportive of anyone. It's become more of a problem than an aid. People lose their jobs and experience a lot of mental stress and mental health issues. There is too much pressure when you have no time and a lot of responsibility, and then you receive little benefit for so much hard work. It's not convenient at all. Samsara is a roller coaster where you can never maintain your feelings, never maintain your thoughts, and never maintain your stability of mind. When you are unhappy, you immediately reject that feeling, and when you are happy, you want to maintain that feeling permanently. But that approach is impossible, so you need to change that attitude. When you are happy, know that your happiness will change. You may be happy now, but that happiness won't stay, and that's fine. When you are not happy, you don't need to reject the cause of your unhappiness. Just say, "Okay, back to normal, not very happy again." We know that feelings switch all the time. We need to understand each other in exactly this way, too, as couples, as friends, and as families, but especially as parents and children.

MODERN FAMILIES

It can be very difficult and challenging to integrate family life with spiritual practice. It takes a lot of skill. We have been pulled into a materialistic view where it's difficult to believe in religion and your family members may have no interest in spirituality. They may be more interested in the material world. If you challenge their beliefs, they might think you are mad, so don't get surprised if their reaction is less than what you would hope for. We are trying to balance two worlds without letting it get too rocky when we follow our spiritual path, so we need to keep it calm. If you can maintain a good balance, your family life and your spiritual practice will both be firm. Modern families have so many commitments—house insurance, health insurance, car registration, telephone bills, technology upgrades, taxes, and mortgages. It's so much to maintain! But we have to work hard to do so because it is all necessary in this modern life. Then, when you have obstacles or problems in your family and make a big deal out of them—whether you're not happy, you're stressed, or want to change things—this is just adding stress onto stress.

When couples look after each other, sharing the childcare, sharing their suffering and happiness, we call it a family. Being a family is not just about saying to your partner, "Oh, we need to have kids," like you are starting a business. Children are not a business, so you shouldn't think of them as a necessity. It's up to you. Once you have kids, you need to take care of them as much as possible. Of course, some people care for their kids too much and spoil them, while others do nothing. Some kind of balance is helpful.

If someone in your life or your family takes advantage of your kindness, you might think, "Why are they being hard on me? They must think I'm weak." However, kindness is not weakness. Unkind people may look more successful, but they're really not; they may just be taking advantage of others, that's all. If someone takes advantage of you, choose that moment to practice. That kind of behavior is no good for them and it's no good for you. One person being grounded like this can make a real difference to the general atmosphere. Letting go is a very good practice. If something is impossible, accept that and let go. Don't try to make it possible. Try your best, but if it doesn't work out, it's time to drop it.

When you have stress or pressure in the home, just listen to the situation; feel it and see it, but don't get stressed by stress. When the mind is calm, it's much easier to communicate because you can talk better and hear better. You are not just listening to your own stress, to your own mind. If you just talk because you are stressed, you put everything in the same mental file of what you believe. You just open the file and put everything in. But this is not your file. You need to rest the mind and cancel that file, you don't need it. If you really listen from your heart rather than your mind, you will get a clear understanding of the situation.

PARTNERSHIPS

Life is demanding and relationships are not easy. Sometimes a relationship may feel like putting two minds together in a cage, but if that happens for you, don't make a big deal out of it; you just need to find balance within it. Don't take your thoughts and feelings too seriously or you will just make yourself and other people uneasy. Relationships are impermanent, and there's no such thing as a friendship that never changes. Some relationships may last longer than others, because each person has different karma.

When we are in a relationship, we should try to enjoy each other's company even when there is conflict because conflict is just a part of life. We find it difficult to enjoy conflicts if we think, "I'm right, you're wrong. Why are you telling me I'm wrong!" Yet we always debate like that. In the end, it's quite boring, because nobody is right. We are all wrong. You need to stop looking for right or wrong, because even if everything ends up right, there will be no peace. There might be order and rules, but they won't function. What we are really looking for is peace. It doesn't matter if something is wrong if it brings peace. Wrong or right is not the point, these are just judgments anyway. Something may be right for you and wrong for someone else, so don't get stressed by things; just have fun as a couple, as a family, as friends. If one person is grumpy, the other person should practice patience. You can switch from time to time and say, "Yesterday you were grumpy so today it's my turn."

There needs to be a lot of communication around the disagreements and arguments in your life, but in the end, there should be only one aim. We have the right to discuss our issues, and we can discuss them and disagree, but in the end, we should have one goal: to be accommodating to your partner, just as they should be accommodating to you. We tend to think, "My brass is gold and their gold is brass." That is the collective way of thinking. Reverse that attitude and trust the way it is. Do you trust yourself? No. You do whatever you want, and your mind drives you crazy. You can't trust this mind, but you still do, you still follow it!

Often what happens is that for the first few years of a marriage, you think your partner is an angel, then after some years have passed, you think they are the devil and get divorced. There is a joke that marriage has three rings: an engagement ring, a wedding ring, and suffering. We can't change that; it's the nature of samsara, everyone's relationship has the same problems. The question is how do you deal with your partner when they make you upset? Should you lie in wait to make them upset in return? That's what people often do. We need to accept that to be upset is part of life. Rejecting the things that upset us is the mind game that we play; we tell ourselves, "I am right, they are wrong." We take small problems and make them big.

Everybody has different policies and different wishes, which is why it's good to understand each other. If your partner is interested in sports or going to the spa or has a different hobby than you, it's important to let them enjoy that kind of fun. If they like playing football or going shopping or doing something you think is crazy, let them do it. Everybody needs something fun to do. Let them enjoy that. Then you will be communicating so well and giving freedom to each other. Understanding each other is important. That might sound simple, but it's not.

Try not to add to your stress by refusing to accept the conditioned nature of relationships. That's life. It's just a process of learning. You will maintain your relationship with more fun rather than more stress if you can accept that. It is important to understand that one mind is not easy and two minds together are very difficult; so how are you going to make it fun? That will depend on whether both of you learn to rest your mind and try to understand and support each other. Then you can say, "Okay, you go," and the other person will say, "No, you go." You will both have freedom.

MODERN PARENTING

Parenting is a big challenge. It is the responsibility of parents to take care of their children if they want a say in the kind of people they will become. We need to look after our children as small kids, teenagers, and young adults. Kids have their own limited needs, teenagers have their own wishes, and young adults have their own views. There are a lot of stages to go through. Their future and the kind of parents they will become depends on how you raise them. It's important to raise a community and not just a child, because children are the future of a country. The kind of country we will have depends on how we raise our children now. We can look at kids in the streets and see what their future will be; we can predict that.

We need to discipline our kids a little bit, but not the kind of stupid discipline used during ancient times, or maybe in your own childhood. There are two ways to teach community culture: through control and through discipline. These are very different things. In the modern world, we try to control everything, but that is not discipline. Discipline must come from self-discipline because people need to realize things for themselves. That involves some fear of consequences so that kids see the threshold of what is acceptable and don't want to cross it. This is not about corporeal punishment but about constantly maintaining dignity. A bit of discipline helps things to run smoothly. You don't need to yell at each other all the time.

In Asian countries, some kids are a little scared of their parents because the parents smack them. That is not a good approach to discipline, however, because the kids don't really understand what they are doing wrong. Kids need to know the reason; they need the discipline and the rationale for the discipline. There are two sides of the coin here: in the West, kids have too much freedom; and in the East, the discipline is a bit too tough. We need to find a balance.

Parents want to do the best for their kids, but kids don't understand that and parents are often disappointed. The parent feels they are doing their best, but their children don't get it. The problem is it's too early for them to get it, so rather than suffer because of that, you need to understand that they don't want to get it. If you wait for them to get it, they will. That is your role as a parent anyway. It doesn't matter if your kids are happy about what you are doing or not, or if they recognize that you are supporting them or not, it's your duty as a parent to do the best for them. Sometimes duty is quite tough.

Parenting is a big responsibility, it's a big practice, a full-time job. Kids aren't always easy, but that's not wrong, that's their job. Kids need to cry and parents need to listen. There is nothing wrong with that, it's part of life. It just means we must be responsible along with having fun. I'm not saying kids are very difficult and parents are always good. Kids also have a right to feel sad, to feel happy, and to be difficult sometimes; that's the nature of being human.

We also have the modern problem of technology, which is driving our kids crazy. They can stay for hours and hours with their tablets and mobile phones, without even looking up to see the forest or the blue sky. They don't go outside to breathe the air, but we can't blame them; it was our generation that created this. We had a good motivation in doing so, but maybe introducing it to our children wasn't a good idea.

Premodern Parenting

In my childhood, parents hardly looked after their children because the whole community was looking after them. The parents could relax fully, but now that's impossible. My parents were very lucky. They had help from aunties and uncles and other relatives and friends who were good, reliable people and all came to help. Now there are only the parents to run the whole family. Just the two of them, there are no uncles or aunties or grandparents; nobody has any time. Even the parents have no time because they must work. It's quite miraculous how modern families can raise kids and work at the same time.

I'm not saying my childhood was better, it was just different, and I was not aware of any great stress on my parents. I never even heard of stress when I lived in India. I only became aware of it when I went to Europe in 1985. I would listen to people talking and ask, "What is stress? What is burnout? What does it mean to be depressed?" Everybody asked me, "How do you feel?" It was quite interesting to hear someone taking an interest in my feelings. Nobody had ever asked me that before.

My parents were very clever; they took care of us, but not too much and not too little. They gave us only what we needed. I didn't experience any teenage anger, with thoughts of "I want to break everything. I want to be able to do what I want!" I never had that chance. In my generation, we didn't have technology like the internet or computers. We also didn't need it. I would always play by myself in a field while my parents were busy with meetings. They would call me in for lunch and I had to be on time and behave properly. I just climbed trees and played with rocks and wood and mud by the river. It was a wonderful way to grow up. My parents were completely free of parenting responsibilities, they had nothing to do.

THE DZOGCHEN APPROACH

We try to protect our children and prevent them from doing the wrong things so they can learn something, but that can be quite a difficult situation. We need to be kind and patient so we don't hurt them. When they don't want to hear what we're saying or they don't get it, we have to be patient with that, too. If you challenge them, you might end up feeling guilty if it looks like you have done something wrong. It's a difficult balance. If kids don't listen, what can you do? They listen to their own minds; they listen to their own wishes and their own beliefs, not to what is right or wrong. That's how they are. They don't have much of a view. Sometimes they do and sometimes they don't, but that's up to them, we can't choose for them.

The kids must go to school, to the gym, the swimming pool, someone's birthday party, the shopping center, their friend's house, and so on and so forth. Where is the time for the parents in all this? They are completely exhausted. Parents need to make their kids happy, but they should not forget themselves if they want to stay in good health. The kids may be completely wonderful, but if they are happy and able to do whatever they want while you are depressed; that is unfair. We need to have a balance. Balance is very important.

As parents, we need to maintain a kind of dignity that helps us run smoothly, instead of losing composure and yelling at our children. We don't need to yell at the kids and the kids don't need to yell at the parents. When parents are calm, the kids can be calm. When parents panic, when they shout and scream and listen to loud music, or when they look at social media with its inane stories, kids will copy that behavior. You will invite them into that environment and they will become wild. If the parents are calm, the kids may be a bit wild temporarily, but the peaceful atmosphere of the home will give them no way to be crazy. That's a simple way to look after children without being too challenging toward them.

I am the father of five children, so I know the stages, from baby to teenager and beyond. What I have experienced is that it's good to enjoy every moment of that parenting time. My children try my patience but I just accept that this is how it is. I'm not always happy, but that's okay. I accept it, so it's no problem. Life can be boring and repetitive. The nature of samsara is change, there are always causes and conditions at play, so we should just accept whatever happens. Things happen due to a karmic plan, and on top of that, children come with their own karma. If we take the Dzogchen view, everything becomes quite relaxing, even chaos and disasters are not seen as a big deal.

To practice Dzogchen, it is not necessary that you give up samsara. We don't need to become monks and nuns, we don't need to become something different from what we are. We can stay in samsara, but we need to change internally. We need to change our minds. Let go of holding on to "me" and "mine." It's too stressful if you're going around saying, "This is me; this belongs to me, this is mine." You can still have things, don't get me wrong—you can have a beautiful house, a beautiful family, a beautiful car. I'm not saying you need to get rid of that. Renunciation has nothing to do with Dzogchen. In the nuclear family model, you should share your happiness and problems. Look after each other and look after your kids without spoiling them. Balance is the key.

CHAPTER 23

Magical Display

You discover the illusion of mind when you
destroy the house of thought.

ONLY A DREAM

BUDDHISM VIEWS our reality in terms of relative truth and absolute truth. The main point of its philosophy is to help you know the relative structures, but that is quite limited wisdom. Relative truth is only fake news that is appearing as truth. Absolute truth is what is real. However, we must begin by learning the relative view because we believe so firmly in our youth, aging, and death, and in being lost and confused. We might analyze phenomena, but what we see will depend on the relative structure in which our mind creates things and we believe in them. This creates the karmic seeds that keep us spinning in samsara. It's never going to end. The absolute view says there is nothing to watch and no one to watch it. This is not a made-up truth; it's how things have always been. It's the genuine truth. Dzogchen is more or less all absolute truth. We live in an illusory world and we have to break the habit of believing in it. We need to break the habit of believing in the relative, intellectual mind. We are very much part of this illusion because we see, hear, smell, taste, and touch things but fail to recognize that they are not real.

We can understand this with the analogy of dreams. We fall asleep and have experiences in dreams, then wake up, and the experience is gone. It was just a dream. The power of the relative is like a dream that we haven't woken up from yet. We are still sleeping in ignorance. All our suffering, fear, and doubt is only a dream, but our relative view makes us very serious. We follow rules to feel safer, but this is a limited view. You need to recognize that life is all just the magical display of mind. You need to experience every day as a dream. It's hard for us to believe that, because we have such deeply ingrained habits, but you need to keep telling yourself, "I'm in a dream, I'm in a dream." You will still be dreaming, but you need to keep reminding yourself within the dream that you are dreaming.

THE ILLUSION OF MIND

We take everything so seriously, which is probably our biggest issue at the moment. Other Buddhist schools see this as a problem of the karmic structure, but Dzogchen is not interested in karma. According to Dzogchen, all we need to do is stop following our thoughts and see them as the magical display of mind. When you follow your thoughts, you believe that whatever you see and hear is outside you and you don't recognize it as illusion. You hear a bird and think, "It's outside the window." No, it's in the mind.

You discover the illusion of mind when you destroy the house of thought. Everything is illusion, so it doesn't matter what happens, but we do live in the relative world and so until our intellectual mind stops, everything will bother us. We are brainwashed by our illusory experiences and suffer from loss, relationship issues, and health issues. If you could see your relationships as illusion, they would not bother you. Even death is an illusion. All good and bad things in life are illusion.

If someone makes you upset, what should you do? Just see the entire situation as an illusion, from top to bottom. You need to recognize it as the magical display of your mind. Our belief that the illusion is real is the root of all our problems. We get affected by our experiences because our mind tells us they are real, and then we make everything so serious in response. Our intellectual mind creates what we see and keeps pulling us deeply into samsara, to the point where we get completely lost in the experience. That's how it is. Dzogchen calls this "the illusion of mind." We are one hundred percent influenced by our intellectual mind. That is our issue.

We need to regard ignorance, attachment, and hatred—the three poisons at the center of this spinning cycle of samsara—as a magical illusion, because emotions are baseless, rootless, and groundless. If you feel angry, recognize that and ask yourself, "Where does this anger come from? Where does it stay? Where does it go?" It comes from nowhere, it dwells nowhere, it goes nowhere. When you see this, your anger will dissolve by itself. In Dzogchen, our suffering is not the problem, our real problem is failing to recognize that illusion is illusion.

Recall the story of the Indian magician, who conjured the image of lions from sticks and stones. The mesmerized crowd saw the lions and believed they were real; the magician saw the lions, but didn't believe their reality; and the latecomer didn't see anything but sticks and stones. We are like the crowd that sees and believes everything is real and we need to get to the stage where we don't believe it to be real anymore. Meditation is what helps us break the power of illusion. We need to see reality as it is. Ninety percent of people just believe the magic show. Even scientists and technologists can't explain phenomena. The relative world is only a magical display that has been created by mind.

In Dzogchen, there are two forms of magic. The first is *marigpa*, a Tibetan term meaning ignorance. This comes from not recognizing and leads to samsara. The second is *rigpa*, or nondual pure awareness. This comes from recognizing and it leads to enlightenment. Not recognizing is the magic of mind. Recognizing is the magic of pure awareness. The mind is as different from the state of rigpa as dreams are from being awake.

RELATIVE MIND

We can understand the five senses as an app that we have created and downloaded into our intellectual mind. This app needs to keep running for us to function and it makes us believe that all our experiences are real. It is working quite well. Without this app, we could not see, hear, smell, touch, or taste. But we don't how the app works. Nobody does. It's like making a video call on the internet; nobody can explain exactly how it works, not even scientists. People wrote some sort of code and now somehow the whole system works.

Our brain is very easily influenced. It's said that if you tell a person something multiple times, the brain will start to believe it. Mind is there too, don't get me wrong, but mind is separate from the brain. The brain is interesting; if you go to the airport and get on an escalator, the brain just assumes it will do what it always does and move forward. Sometimes the escalator doesn't work but your brain tells you to keep walking and you almost fall. You look at the escalator and get a headache because your brain doesn't know what's going on. It's supposed to move, but it's not moving, and it takes a moment for the brain to register this.

The brain likes to operate on automatic. It registers things in a habitual way. The brain is hardwired like that. Mind is not always alert because it relies on the brain. Dzogchen introduces us to the understanding that all phenomena is an illusion, but from a relative perspective, we are able see it and experience it. We are affected by these experiences because our brain is reading them as real and telling our body, "Yes, this is how it is." We interact through the senses and interpret those interactions through our consciousness. That's how we develop experiences like hot and cold, horrible and nice, beautiful and repulsive. Everything is experienced through the senses. Without them, we would have no karma.

It's essential to start examining these things. You hear a sound and believe it's a sound, smell an odor and believe it's a smell, eat something and believe it's a taste. The senses report back to the mind. It's helpful to remember that the mind is like a monkey in a room with five windows; we forget we are just following this crazy mind and believe everything it says. We completely rely on it and have no control. It can drive you nuts sometimes; you think, "Somebody talked to me badly, it made me so angry. Somebody talked to me nicely, it made me feel great." There are so many thoughts and emotions the mind can pick and choose between. We become very selective and stick to our habitual responses.

We need to stop seeing things through our habitual beliefs and start to see life as it is.

TRICKS OF THE MIND

For something to be an illusion it has to be fake. In Dzogchen, illusion is a thought that arises because we fail to recognize an appearance just as it is and believe it to be real. We don't see the world as it is because we project a different reality onto it. For example, some people are afraid of snakes. You might see a black rope at night and think it's a snake, then you warn your friends and make everyone afraid of the snake. It looks like a snake, so everybody has this fear. Then someone takes a flashlight and shines it on the rope. Now everyone can see it's just a rope. The fear of the snake is gone. Where was the snake—in the rope or in your mind?

The relative view is to see that the rope is not a snake, the rope is just a rope. That is right view because it cuts through fear. To believe the rope is a snake is the nature of samsara. Television and social media are all telling you the rope is a snake, so be careful! When you realize the rope is not a snake, you are not confused anymore. You can see the relative as it is. We can also examine this on a deeper level and ask, "Is that really a rope?" No, it's not even a rope; that is also an illusion. The genuine view is to see that the rope is not even a rope, forget about it being a snake. It is to be able to say, "I am not there, my mind is not there, the rope is not there." We usually just believe these things exist. This is how we are confused.

Once you have this view, there is nothing to worry about. When you cut through the belief that the rope is real, the fear that the rope is a snake will also be gone. You will recognize everything as illusion. Fear makes us block things from our understanding of reality, it traps and imprisons us, and it freezes our perspective. The illusion of mind is created by our failure to recognize a thought just as it is. We have to turn our mind inward and watch our thoughts, because thoughts and their projections do not exist apart from the mind, they are created by the mind.

We are very much part of this illusion and need to stop finding our comfort zone there. We are stuck in a chain of suffering that never ends. When you see a rainbow in the sky, you can't catch it or refuse to see it, but you can learn to see it as it is. When we watch small children together, we don't take it seriously when they fight as they play. We just look at them and laugh. Sometimes we get upset and make a big deal out of our jealousy, anger, miscommunication, and ill health, but we should view our adult dramas in the same way that we view children playing.

NONDUALITY

Recall the analogy of the one moon in the sky reflected in the thousands of lakes on the earth. There appear to be thousands of moons because each lake has its own moon. We all appear to be separate in the same way, and we operate in the world thinking, "This is my moon, this is my lake; that is your moon, that is your lake. That is my friend's moon, this is my enemy's moon." But there is only one moon. We think our moon is better than another person's moon, but it's the same moon. We argue with each other, we criticize each other, we judge each other, but we are all part of that one moon. Dzogchen is a unity, but we believe we are separate and get confused. Separation is an illusion. We need to rediscover our nondual pure awareness. Dzogchen is not creating something you need to believe; belief will come spontaneously because that is how it is.

The Dzogchen teachings say that mind has one ground and two paths. Mind is the ground and we can either take the path of recognizing mind or we can take the path of not recognizing mind. When you recognize mind, you go to enlightenment. When you don't recognize it, you go to samsara. We are used to going to samsara because we have gone down that path so many times. If we had an app that could track the enlightenment path and the samsaric path, we would see thousands of people in a traffic jam on the samsaric path and just a few people on the enlightenment path. This doesn't mean something is wrong, it's just how we are; we follow our minds and believe our old habits.

Dzogchen has very powerful skills and methods to help us break our

habits. Like Manjushri's wisdom sword, they cut through the ignorance
that believes the habits, they cut through the chains of thought. You will
be led by clarity rather than the artificial intellect of this very tiresome
mind. We are so sensitive, grumpy, and emotional and we change from
one day to the next. It's quite boring. Why don't you just go to enlightenment? You can be at peace in everlasting happiness. You don't need to
do anything, you don't need insurance or maintenance. There is no cost.
But you say, "Oh, it's too difficult, enlightenment is impossible." It is not
difficult. Enlightenment isn't far away at all.

In Dzogchen, we go directly to the cause—we cut our problem at the
root instead of cutting off the branches. A tree will still live if you just
cut its branches, but not if you cut it at the root. Likewise, if we only
change certain habits and beliefs, our problems will continue, but if we
cut them all off at the root, they will completely disappear. The root of
all our problems is the mind. It is all one system, a mental system, that
creates the illusion of our lives.

To realize the truth of absolute reality is to go beyond this mind and
beyond illusion. We are not trying to create anything new because we
already have what we're looking for, we are already enlightened. You
currently don't believe that you are who you are. You feel you need to
prove you are buddha with your mind, but this is what prevents you
from recognizing that you are born buddha, you are naturally buddha.
Dzogchen is a limitless view. It is beyond right and wrong. It is beyond
logic. It is complete freedom. With this view you will go to the real, absolute state rather than remaining trapped within an artificial, mind-made
structure. You will no longer be relying on this limiting mental system.
The truth is completely different. It is an incredible view. That is what
we call Dzogchen.

CHAPTER 24

Daily Meditation

Whenever you use the mind,
clarity is far away, so let the mind rest.

STRUCTURED TIME

IT'S GOOD to give yourself time and space each day for meditation. We need to settle the mind and make it calm. There seems to be so much to worry about these days, wherever you go everybody panics, but this only happens because we follow the mind too much. Mind creates all the stress. If we follow the heart, there will be no stress at all. When the mind is calm and settled, we create a gap, and this gap creates an opportunity for the heart to lead. You can combine everything you do with meditation, but it will benefit you to set up a structured time to meditate when you are starting out. Begin with one meditation session each day and you will gradually learn to meditate in every moment. You'll be able to meditate when you're having breakfast. A delicious meal is on the table, you concentrate on it in the present moment, and eat it. As you enjoy the taste, your body, mind, and breakfast are together. It's incredible fun.

CLARITY

Our aim in Dzogchen meditation is to rest the mind in the perfect gap as often as possible. This moment of the gap is peace, but it is hard to maintain it for too long because the mind is so easily distracted. As you continue with this meditation, practice holding your out-breath and resting in the pause for longer periods. You will find clarity within that gap. If you actively look for clarity, you will never find it, but if you follow this method of resting, you will find it. The mind is very tricky, it always says, "I want to look for that," and it tries to manipulate you into imagining where you might get it, but that's impossible. Whenever you use the mind, clarity is far away, so let the mind rest.

Dzogchen meditation is not the technique of breathing in and out; the real meditation is when you pause the breath and rest in the gap. Breathing in and out is just the skillful method for resting. The gap is the meditation. The more you can hold the gap, the better your meditation. This is so simple, you can do it anytime. Whenever you experience stress or difficulties, you can do this meditation for a few minutes. It can change your experience of the situation completely, on the spot.

KEEP IT SIMPLE

Regarding your posture, having your hands apart can almost bring calm to the mind by itself, because it prevents the development of thoughts. This is a Dzogchen insight into the meditation posture. Just putting your hands on your knees does the job. It's incredible and very simple. In some meditation styles you are required to sit in the lotus posture, but that can be quite painful, so just sit on the floor or in a chair and rest your hands on your knees. Keep your breathing very gentle and slow. This slow breathing is called "Dzogchen breathing," and it is a healing way of breathing. Breathe in slowly and gently, then breathe out slowly and gently. Just breathe in and out, in and out, through the mouth, not the nostrils. From time to time, you can focus your attention on the breath and follow that flow.

It can be quite beneficial to do this meditation by the ocean or on a mountain because you will have an unobstructed view of the open sky. Don't worry about anything you see—birds, airplanes, people selling ice cream. Don't follow any of that. Just let it go. Looking into the blue sky is nice. Look to the west in the morning and to the east in the evening because then you will have the sun at your back and not in your eyes. Breathe slowly from the mouth. It's important to have your eyes open and looking directly ahead; don't look down, don't look up, just enjoy the space. And don't worry. There are absolutely no worries. Just enjoy it and breathe.

THE MEDITATION SESSION

Dzogchen instructions for meditation are very simple. We discussed the posture and methods in some detail in earlier chapters, so this summary is meant as an easy reference for your daily practice when you need a quick refresher.

It helps to set aside a suitable time each day for meditation and to break your session into several five-minute mini-sessions with a short break between each one to keep it fresh and clear. Begin with relative shamatha for a few short sessions and then do one or two sessions of Dzogchen shamatha. From time to time, you can also do a short session of analytical meditation; instructions for this are included at the end of the instructions below.

The posture

Sit comfortably on a cushion or a chair with your hands resting on your knees. Keep your spine straight and lean back slightly. Your shoulders should be relaxed. Take a minute to settle comfortably into the posture. Keep your eyes open, look straight ahead, and breathe slowly in and out through your open mouth, not through your nostrils.

Relative shamatha: Meditation with an object

Concentrate your mind on an object, such as a potted plant, a rock, or an image of the Buddha or a wisdom deity. Look directly at the object and focus your attention on it. Whenever you drift off into thoughts of the three times, use that object as an anchor to bring your awareness back into the present moment.

Relative shamatha: Meditation without an object

Begin by focusing on the object of your choice in meditation, paying attention to all its details. Close your eyes and recall those details so that you can visualize the object clearly.

Relative shamatha: Staying in the present moment

Don't follow thoughts about the past. Don't follow thoughts about the future. Rest in the present moment.

Relative shamatha: Let come, let go

Recognize each thought as it arises, but do not block it and do not follow it. Just let it come and let it go. Let it arise without either trying to repress, deny, or disown it or trying to grasp onto it. Then let it go without judgment, without creating a narrative around it, and without following or solidifying the emotions that surround it.

Learn to see your habitual thoughts and emotions as old friends. If you simply let thoughts come and let them go, they will gradually resolve by themselves. When you give up the habit of being bothered by them, you will recognize they are just like thieves in an empty house. They can't hurt someone who isn't there.

Dzogchen shamatha: Resting the mind

Breathe in and out through the mouth, then hold the out-breath for a few seconds. It creates a gap between thoughts when your breathing stops. Rest your mind in that gap for a few seconds. Repeat this breathing cycle for a few minutes, then take a short break from the meditation. Relax and adjust your posture for a minute, then start the cycle of breathing again.

You can repeat this cycle of resting three or four times, keeping the sessions short and sharp so that the mind does not have a chance to settle into dullness.

Investigation

Investigate the reality of things in a series of meditation exercises. Start by investigating the self by focusing on the "I," the mind, and the senses and asking a series of questions about them. Then investigate external phenomena by asking the same series of questions:

Where does it come from?

Where does it stay?

Where does it go?

CHAPTER 25

Conclusion

You always bring your mind to your meditation experience, but if you don't assign any role to your mind, everything will drop away.

CONTINUITY

WHAT IS the real purpose of your life? To rest the mind. When we do this, all the things you need and want in life—such as good health, wealth, fun, or anything else—will be maintained on the relative level. If you have a mobile phone, you need to recharge the battery every day. We also need to recharge our energy every day. Meditation is a great way to recharge, and if you maintain it, the purpose of your life will be maintained, too. You always bring your mind to your meditation experience, but if you don't assign any role to your mind, everything will drop away. When you are resting the mind, you don't need to bring your intellectual mind along to label or analyze your experiences. We always bring our old socks. Meditation is not about trying to drop your old habits, it's just about resting the mind. Just wear your fresh socks and be completely clear and pure and without thought. It's important to remain like that.

Meditation is a training. To become skilled at anything, you need to train in it. Real meditation is this continuity. We need to practice it every day. You don't need to look for answers or solutions; just practice meditation and you will break the habit of seeing appearances through your beliefs, habits, and prejudices. Continuity is the most important aspect of meditation practice. You are creating a new habit by turning your mind toward stillness. Don't fight your mind when it resists, you can't push it by saying, "I want to experience certain things in meditation." Mind loves the drama; it loves it when you are stressed or discouraged. Every meditator experiences obstacles. When the mind resists, meditation stops being as easy as it was at the beginning. These obstacles are quite common, and you will get past them. They are not such a big deal.

We need to calm the mind that keeps analyzing, researching, and looking for something. Stop looking and rest. You will become spontaneous, which is an experience that cannot be produced by mind. An academic education will not give it to you. It will only arise when the intellect and its thoughts are completely shut down. Some people think they can just do a university course to understand Dzogchen, but it's not an academic subject, it is one hundred percent an individual experience. Dzogchen can't be found through a search engine. Dzogchen is passed down in a lineage from teacher to student, so you need to be part of a lineage to really get it.

Some people might say, "Oh, I like Dzogchen, it's incredible," but they just use this view to promote themselves. That is no good. You don't need to promote yourself. If you have the right view, it will promote itself. Buddhism is not about trying to be someone. Buddhism is trying to show you who you already are, the ultimate genuine you, so that you become a genuine person. There is no need to build this artificially.

The more you rest your mind, the more you will see your life as a dream. It will become less serious and you will have less stress and doubt because those things come from believing things to be real. When you rest the mind, the reality of things can become so subtle, there is almost nowhere to get caught in believing things like, "This is who I am," or following emotions, stress, or doubt. All that will be gone. If you keep doing this practice without giving up, you will progress day by day.

Life is extremely precious, but it's not permanent, so don't miss your opportunity to use it for its real purpose. Put the effort into your meditation and don't get distracted by the small things. You can achieve something incredible in this lifetime, but if you miss the opportunity, it might be impossible to find it again. What is the benefit of recognizing your buddha nature? Everlasting peace. We work so hard in samsara, but our pleasures only last a short time. Why not choose enlightenment? It's calm and incredible and where all stress is gone.

NINE VEHICLES

We get a good view if we climb a small hill and a slightly better view if we climb a higher hill. If you go to another even higher hill, you will get a better view again. The Nyingma school of Tibetan Buddhism has nine vehicles, where each vehicle has a higher view than the previous one. This classification isn't to say one vehicle is better than the others, it just refers to the view each vehicle will give you. Dzogchen is the ninth vehicle and it will give you the highest view of all. Every other view is subsumed within Dzogchen, so you will not be missing anything if you have this view. All the other views are good too, they just don't see as far. Dzogchen is the ultimate view, the deepest, simplest, and most practical view. If you can get this view, it's good enough, you don't need more than that.

You may need to have another view first before you can get to the Dzogchen view or you may just go direct to Dzogchen. You have that choice. Some people progress in a gradual fashion until they reach the Dzogchen view, while others take a shortcut straight to it. It depends on your individual situation, although it's not exactly a choice one makes, because it depends upon your capacity and whether you have the skills or not. If you are interested in cooking, gardening, or carpentry, you will pick up the necessary skills quickly because of your motivation and experience. You will be successful at it because of your skill. The experience will feel quite stable, grounded, and powerful, but you can't attain that feeling without skill. You need to be guided and you also need to make choices. You need to listen and learn because that will give you a deeper understanding. It will help you to understand things completely differently.

This is not a criticism of other views; this just concerns the steps one makes toward the highest view. There are steps one, two, and three up to steps eight and nine. Progressing in a gradual fashion will help you not to harm each other, because if you are at step nine and you are relating to someone at step one, you are not supposed to be surprised when that person doesn't have the same view as you. You can't judge them for having a more limited view. It doesn't mean they won't one day be at the higher level. They won't stay at step one forever; they are just going through a process that takes time.

Tibetan Buddhism has four schools: the Nyingma, Kagyu, Sakya, and Gelug. The Nyingma is the oldest of these and has six major lineages of its own, each with its own monastery and hundreds of branch monasteries. Dzogchen originated in India and belongs to the Nyingma school. It was maintained the most properly at Dzogchen Monastery in Tibet; the other schools didn't particularly maintain it. Dzogchen Monastery was highly successful at the time of the great Fourth Dzogchen Rinpoche, Mingyur Namkhai Dorje (1793–1870), when Patrul Rinpoche resided at the monastery. It was like a second Nalanda University, the famed center of monastic education in ancient India. Dzogchen Rinpoche gave introduction to the other Nyingma lineages at Katok, Dorje Drak, Palyul, Mindrolling, and Shechen monasteries, so all the Dzogchen teachings and lineages taught in Nyingma monasteries come from Dzogchen Monastery.

ALREADY BUDDHA

The legacy that comes down through these great masters at Dzogchen Monastery is that there is nowhere to go to get enlightenment. Enlightenment is who you really are. It was never born and never dies. People say they aren't ready for buddhahood, but enlightenment is already ready, you don't need to make it ready. You believe your ideas about yourself and assume enlightenment is difficult, but enlightenment is not difficult—you are difficult. Enlightenment is there within you all the time. When you recognize who you are, you cut the root of illusion. The trouble is you never go there. You might understand the idea of who you are, but you keep going back to believing in fake reality, because the illusion of mind won't let you recognize how it really is. If you break the illusion, you are buddha. Although the failure to recognize that you are buddha is also an illusion.

We need more obstacles and more suffering because they are fuel for the fire of wisdom. We are currently one hundred percent influenced by mind; we are brainwashed by mind. When you attain realization, your emotions just become energy; they don't disappear, but their purpose changes. Before enlightenment, emotions are led by ignorance, but after enlightenment, they are led by wisdom. Buddha nature belongs to all sentient beings, not just to buddhas. All you need to do is recognize this buddha nature as perfect already. You don't need to make it better, you don't need to make it worse, just leave it as it is. What is missing from your life? Only this recognition. The only reason Dzogchen has all these meditation stages is to help you get to this recognition.

Please enjoy your life. Whether you are thirty, forty, or one hundred years old, you should have fun and enjoy every second of your life. Don't worry about when you are going to die. Death will come whether you worry or not. Worry is not going to make your life longer or shorter, so forget about it. The best way to enjoy things is through meditation and doing everything from your heart. If something in your life doesn't work out the way you want, then leave it alone. Let it go, don't keep pushing for outcomes all the time. Stop worrying about the little things and worry about big things like enlightenment. Enlightenment is easy, it's only you that is difficult. You need to make yourself easy. You are already enlightened, you don't need to look for ways to get enlightened. You are already pure, you don't need to become pure. Everybody has this pure awareness. Every sentient being has it. You have the best thing already, you have what you need. Just let go and rest the mind; your pure awareness will be there. Don't look for it because it's there already. That's it! You have won the lottery. Your pure awareness is within you.

Glossary

absolute truth. The truth that is beyond everything—beyond explanation, beyond language, beyond action, beyond truth and lies. *See also* two truths; relative truth.

alaya. The relative ground of our experience, the karmic patterns of the mind that determine how we construct our world.

atiyoga. The ninth vehicle (*yana*) in the nine-yana system of the Nyingma school. The Sanskrit equivalent for the Tibetan term *Dzogchen*, it means "ultimate" yoga and contains the highest wisdom of Tibetan Buddhism.

buddha. A buddha is someone who has overcome all obscurations and achieved everlasting happiness.

buddha nature. The completely perfect and pure nature that is born within every sentient being, the wisdom born within us and with us all the time.

Do Khyentse Yeshe Dorje (1800–66). Regarded as the mind emanation of Jigme Lingpa, he demonstrated the power of his enlightened mind by performing such acts as vanishing for days to pure lands, bringing murdered beings back to life, and leaving imprints of his body on rocks. He famously introduced Patrul Rinpoche to the nature of mind while beating him and dragging him by the hair.

Dzogchen. The "Great Perfection," the oldest and highest wisdom lineage within Tibetan Buddhism. The Tibetan equivalent for the Sanskrit term *atiyoga.* An authentic, unbroken lineage of the Nyingma school that has been passed from master to disciple to the present day. It is the excellent teaching for this time and place.

Guru Rinpoche (also *Guru Padmasambhava*). The eighth-century Indian tantric master renowned in Tibet as the second Buddha, who tamed Tibet and brought Buddhism and the Dzogchen teachings from India. It is said that if you pray to Guru Rinpoche, he will never leave you.

Hinayana. One of three major traditions of Buddhism that explains everything in terms of karmic causes and conditions. It focuses on avoiding harm and teaches personal liberation through the renunciation of samsara. *See also* Mahayana; Vajrayana.

hutuktu. A Tibetan title for the rank of highest spiritual significance, a rank second only to the king in Tibet.

Jigme Lingpa (1730–98). A great master of the Nyingma tradition, he was a terton, or discoverer of treasure teachings, and revealed the *Longchen Nyingthig* based on a series of pure visions revealed to him by Longchenpa as mind treasures, which became an important cycle of meditative practice in the Nyingma school.

kadag. Primordial purity from beginningless time, a permanent and unchanging purity that is beyond the dualism of being pure or impure.

Khandro Nyingthig. The "*Heart Essence of the Dakinis*" cycle of teachings that was brought to Tibet by Guru Padmasambhava. He taught it to Yeshe Tsogyal and one hundred thousand wisdom dakinis and then transferred it as a terma into the mind of Princess Pema Sal, King Trisong Detsen's daughter, as she lay dying at the age of eight. It was then written in symbolic script by Yeshe Tsogyal, entrusted to the dakinis, and hidden with the intention to be revealed at a later time.

Kuntuzangpo (Sanskrit: *Samantabhadra*). Depicted as a buddha, sky blue in color, sitting in the expanse of space and encircled by an aura of rainbow light. He is completely naked to show that he is unstained by any trace of concepts. His name means "total goodness" to signify that our true nature is fundamental goodness.

lineage. The transmission of the teachings from teacher to student through a line of the living masters from the time of the Buddha through Nalanda University to today, so that genuine realization is transmitted from one master to another, which preserves the authenticity of those teachings.

Longchen Nyingthig. The *"Heart Essence of the Great Expanse,"* a mind-treasure that was revealed as a terma cycle by Longchenpa to Jigme Lingpa. Longchenpa had condensed the Nyingthig teachings from the *Khandro Nyingthig* and *Vima Nyingthig*, revealed by Vimalamitra, into one cycle of teachings.

Longchenpa (1308–64). A Tibetan yogi-scholar of the Nyingma school, he was the immediate reincarnation of Pema Ledrel Tsal and the indirect incarnation of Princess Pema Sal. He received the *Khandro Nyingthig* back from Pema Ledrel Tsal's disciple Gyalse Lekden, and thus ensured the authentic lineage of the *Khandro Nyingthig* was kept alive. The omniscient Longchenpa was one of the most brilliant and original writers on Tibetan Buddhism. He systematized the Nyingma teachings and wrote extensively on Dzogchen.

Mahayana. One of three major traditions of Buddhism; it goes beyond the liberation of the Hinayana by focusing on cultivating good thoughts and actions and avoiding negative thoughts and actions. It teaches enlightenment is reached by creating merit for countless eons through trying to help others. *See also* Hinayana, Vajrayana.

mala. A "garland" of 108 beads, similar to a rosary, that is used for counting mantra and prayer recitations.

mandala. The Tibetan mandala is a visual tool for generating wisdom and compassion. It is usually depicted as a balanced geometrical shape, a stylized palace where wisdom deities reside. The principal deity is housed in the center.

Manjushri. A deity who wields a flaming sword in his right hand to represent the wisdom that cuts through ignorance. He symbolizes the embodiment of wisdom.

marigpa. Tibetan term for the ignorance that keeps us from recognizing our nondual pure awareness, or *rigpa*, and leads to samsara.

Mingyur Namkhai Dorje, the Fourth Dzogchen Rinpoche (1793–1870). His realization was so special, other masters would spontaneously bow down before him. He had completely transcended all worldly concerns and conventional norms and he became a legend as stories about his supernatural deeds and clairvoyance spread around.

Ngedon Tenzin Zangpo, the Third Dzogchen Rinpoche (1759–92). A terton who could clearly remember his previous lives and wrote the famous commentary on Longchenpa's *Khandro Nyingthig*, entitled *The Excellent Chariot*. He built a retreat center in the upper valley near Dzogchen Monastery in which thirteen of his students attained enlightenment through rainbow body.

nine vehicles. The Nyingma school divides the spiritual path into nine levels or vehicles (Sanskrit: *yana*) for working with the mind. The first three are on sutric levels and the last six are on tantric levels. The final tantric level is Dzogchen, or *atiyoga* in Sanskrit.

nirvana. The state of nirvana is the same as becoming a buddha or realizing one's buddha nature.

Nyingma. The "Old" school or oldest lineage of Tibetan Buddhism, founded on the first lineages and early translations of Buddhist texts from Sanskrit into Tibetan during the eighth century. It has a unique system of nine vehicles in which Dzogchen, one of the original lineages of the Nyingma school, is considered the most direct, profound, and subtle path to enlightenment.

Patrul Rinpoche (1808–87). An enlightened master who lived the life of a vagabond while being one of the most illustrious spiritual teachers of the nineteenth century. He taught for many years at Shri Singha college at Dzogchen Monastery. When he taught Shantideva's *Way of the Bodhisattva* (*Bodhicharyavatara*) at the college, for several years in succession large numbers of flowers called *serchen* blossomed suddenly. They became known as "Bodhicharyavatara flowers."

Pema Ledrel Tsal (thirteenth century). The rebirth of Princess Pema Sal, whom Guru Rinpoche had entrusted the *Khandro Nyingthig* in the eighth century. He withdrew the terma of the *Khandro Nyingthig* from its place of concealment and taught it to his disciple Gyalse Lekden. Pema Ledrel Tsal was reborn as the omniscient Longchenpa.

Pema Rigdzin, the First Dzogchen Rinpoche (1625–97). The founder of the Dzogchen Monastery in Kham, eastern Tibet, in 1684. A mind emanation of the Indian mahasiddhas Vimalamitra, Padmasambhava, and Saraha, he was said to have been Dzogchen personified. *Pema* means "lotus" and *rigdzin* means "awareness holder" or "holder of rigpa."

Princess Pema Sal (eighth century). The daughter of King Trisong Detsen who died suddenly at the age of eight. To console the distraught king, Guru Rinpoche drew the syllable NRI over the princess's heart and brought her back to life with the hook of his awareness. He conferred the cycle of the *Khandro Nyingthig* on her and empowered her to reveal it in a future life. The *Khandro Nyingthig* was then hidden as terma in a cave. The princess was reborn some centuries later as Pema Ledrel Tsal.

protector deities. The protector deities of the Nyingma school have all been subjugated and commanded by Guru Rinpoche to protect the lineages, lineage holders, and followers. These protectors never harm and always protect the lineages.

relative truth. The truth that exists within the bounds of karma and is manifested by mind. Whatever feelings and thoughts we have are within relative truth. The realization of relative truth gives us the platform to recognize what ultimate truth is. *See also* two truths; ultimate truth.

rigpa. The Tibetan term for nondual pure awareness, the true nature of mind, which is always present.

Samantabhadra. See Kuntuzangpo.

samsara. Everyday life with its stress, confusion, temporary happiness, and temporary joy.

seed syllable. A primordial Sanskrit sound that embodies the essence of samsaric realms, buddha realms, and wisdom deities.

serkyem. A Tibetan ritual offering instrument meaning "golden drink," which is a set of two pieces, a chalice set within a basin for overflowing offerings. Commonly filled with tea or alcohol as an offering to local deities and protectors.

shamatha. A form of meditation that reduces stress and confusion by bringing concentration to the present moment without following thoughts about the past or future. *See also* vipashyana.
- *absolute shamatha.* This practice is unique to Dzogchen and entails bringing the mind to complete rest in a state of awareness where all thoughts dissolve, which gives rise to an experience of clarity.
- *relative shamatha.* This practice involves remaining in the present moment by not following thoughts about past or future.
- *shamatha with support* (Tibetan: *ten che*). A form of shamatha that uses the support of an external object to focus the mind in concentration.
- *shamatha without support* (Tibetan: *ten me*). A form of shamatha in which one visualizes an object of support in the imagination, with eyes closed, in order to focus the mind in concentration.

Shantideva (eighth century). An Indian scholar and monk, the renowned author of *The Way of the Bodhisattva*.

shedra. A teaching college on monastic grounds where the education program is conducted.

Shri Singha Shedra. The teaching college at Dzogchen Monastery, it was among the first and was the most famous and influential of Tibetan shedras. Founded in the nineteenth century at the time of the Fourth Dzogchen Rinpoche, Mingyur Namkhai Dorje, it produced many of the finest scholars in Tibet.

stupa. A dome-shaped structure that contains relics (sacred objects or burial remains). It can be a large building that serves as a shrine to be circumambulated as an act of worship or a miniature representation that sits on a shrine as a symbol of the buddha mind.

Tara (Tibetan: *Jetsun Drolma*). Arya Tara is the wisdom goddess or protectress, the embodiment of universal compassion, who is known as the supreme liberator due to her ability to remove obstacles, especially fear and anxiety. She is recognized in all schools of Tibetan Buddhism.

terma. Sacred texts or objects hidden by Guru Rinpoche and Yeshe Tsogyal as treasures in the eighth century for the benefit of future generations. They may be physical objects such as texts or ritual implements buried in the ground, hidden in rocks or crystals, or in the sky or space. A terma may also be a teaching hidden in the mind of the guru.

terton. A treasure revealer, a person who discovers the ancient terma in the earth, rocks, sky, or their own mind. Many tertons are considered incarnations of the twenty-five main disciples of Guru Rinpoche.

two truths. Reality exists at two levels in Buddhism, the level of relative truth and absolute truth. *See also* absolute truth; relative truth.

Vajrayana. A system of tantric practices that developed in India and spread across the Himalayas to places like Tibet, Nepal, and Mongolia. Vajrayana practices are connected to specific lineages in Buddhism through the teachings of lineage holders. *See also* Hinayana; Mahayana.

vipashyana. This refers to the extraordinary view of clarity or insight that is attained through meditation practice and generally arises when the practices of shamatha and meditative investigation are combined together. This view can also arise naturally when you become stabilized in absolute shamatha. *See also* shamatha.

Index

About the Author

His Eminence the Seventh Dzogchen Rinpoche, Jigme Losel Wangpo, is the holder of the Dzogchen lineage. He was born in Sikkim in 1964 into the Lakar Tsang family, a noble family whose connection to the Dzogchen tradition and the great masters of Tibet dates back over many centuries. His Eminence's father was the late Tsewang Paljor, whose family lineage is of terton descent traced back to Dudul Nuden Dorje. Tsewang Paljor was greatly respected and renowned as the private secretary to the second Jamyang Khyentse of Dzongsar, Dorje Chang, Chökyi Lodrö. His Eminence's mother is Pema Tsering Wangmo of the Lakar Tsang family, known as great patrons of Dharma in the Kham region of eastern Tibet.

Around the time of Dzogchen Rinpoche's birth, both parents had many auspicious dreams. There were also many auspicious signs to indicate the incarnation of a great master. Even before his official recognition, many respected lamas came to visit this incredible young boy. His Holiness the Fourth Dodrupchen Rinpoche, Thupten Trinley Palzang, recognized Rinpoche as the Dzogchen lineage holder in a clear pure light vision at the time of his conception, and later performed his enthronement ceremony in Sikkim's Royal Palace in Gangtok on the eighth of October, 1972.

Rinpoche began his spiritual training at the Nyingma Institute, where he received private teachings from Dodrupchen Rinpoche and Khenpo Rahor Thupten. At the age of twelve, Dzogchen Rinpoche was invited to study at the Buddhist School of Dialectics in Dharamsala by His Holiness the Fourteenth Dalai Lama, Tenzin Gyatso, who personally supervised his education. Rinpoche was also instructed by many other great lamas in ritual practice and academic study. Among them were His Holiness Dudjom Rinpoche, His Holiness Dilgo Khyentse Rinpoche, and His Holiness Trulshik Rinpoche. Other senior masters trained Dzogchen Rinpoche in ritual and grammar under the guidance of His Holiness Dodrupchen Rinpoche. Khenpo Tsundu was responsible for his training in Nyingma philosophy, and Khenpo Mewa Thupten gave him the deep philosophical teachings of the Nyingma tradition. Rinpoche also simultaneously undertook Gelug philosophical studies under the guidance of Geshe Lobsang Gyatso. Later on, he received Dzogchen lineage transmission, including the teachings of Longchenpa, from Khenchen Pema Tsewang.

Dzogchen Rinpoche excelled as a scholar and obtained the title of Rabjampa at the age of nineteen. He displayed a great capacity to realize the highest teachings across both the Nyingma and Gelug traditions and was ahead of the rest of his class despite being much younger than his fellow students. This vigorous training prepared Dzogchen Rinpoche for his role of leading Dzogchen Monastery a few years later at the age of twenty-one.

Historically, the Dzogchen Rinpoches have a close connection with the Medicine Buddha, and he is known to have transformed the health of many people. The Seventh Dzogchen Rinpoche's work also has charitable dimensions. Recognized by His Holiness the Dalai Lama and the Tibetan Government in Exile for his outstanding commitment to the welfare of the Tibetan community, Rinpoche has transformed the Dhondenling Tibetan settlement through two decades of community development.

The Dzogchen Rinpoches are known as the guardians of the Dzogchen lineage and are responsible for the preservation of its ancient rituals and teachings. Rinpoche travels the world teaching the Khandro Nyingthig and he preserves the authentic rituals of this wisdom tradition that is so beneficial for the modern world through the activities of Dzogchen Monastery. As holder of one of the remaining unbroken spiritual traditions in the world, His Eminence the Seventh Dzogchen Rinpoche is an authentic guide revealing to us our true nature and showing us, through his example, that we have everything we need within ourselves to unlock our own inherent wisdom.

What to Read Next
from Wisdom Publications

LIBERATION FROM SAMSARA
Oral Instructions on the Preliminary Practices of Longchen Nyingthik
Kyabjé Dodrupchen Rinpoché
Translated by Tulku Thondup Rinpoche and Sonam Paljor Dejongpa

This rare teaching by Rinpoché is a uniquely concise volume of the teachings of the path to liberation that is authentic, authoritative, and complete.

THE NYINGMA SCHOOL OF TIBETAN BUDDHISM
Its Fundamentals and History
Dudjom Rinpoche
Translated and edited by Gyurme Dorje and Matthew Kapstein

"A landmark in the history of English-language studies of Tibetan Buddhism."—*History of Religions*

BEING HUMAN AND A BUDDHA TOO
Longchenpa's Sevenfold Mind Training for a Sunlit Sky
Anne C. Klein

"This is a must for anyone who is interested in Tibetan Buddhism, especially in the key insights of Dzogchen teaching."—Thupten Jinpa, PhD, author and translator of *Essential Mind Training*

About Wisdom Publications

Wisdom Publications is the leading publisher of classic and contemporary Buddhist books and practical works on mindfulness. To learn more about us or to explore our other books, please visit our website at wisdomexperience.org or contact us at the address below.

Wisdom Publications
132 Perry Street
New York, NY 10014 USA

We are a 501(c)(3) organization, and donations in support of our mission are tax deductible.

Wisdom Publications is affiliated with the Foundation for the Preservation of the Mahayana Tradition (FPMT).